MW00938493

Endorsements

"From the tenant perspective when you (Jorge Morales) were representing the owner, you have always been professional and willing to discuss an issue or leasing topic with what came through to me as an open mind looking for a good solution for both parties."
Bill Vornehm, Senior Director Real Estate, WPP Group

"Jorge Morales is not only a real estate professional who understands his business, he cares about his clients. Jorge and I spent many times together discussing my nonprofit's needs as a tenant, which he always proactively sought out. Jorge made it a point to get to know me as a person and as a professional, and I came to see him more as a partner than a landlord. One of the industry's best in my book!"
Alfred Sanchez, President and CEO,
Greater Miami Chamber of Commerce.

"Jorge Morales' expertise and skill was vital to facilitating the lease for NAOE on Brickell Key Island in Miami. Finding an ideal space for our unique restaurant was a daunting task. Jorge was responsive and made the entire leasing process easy for us. A pleasure to work with."
Kevin Cory, Kamakura, Inc., NAOE® Restaurant

"Jorge Morales is a consummate professional in all aspects of his business. From taking care of his client's needs to ensuring that the deals he is involved with happen, Jorge is an excellent commercial real estate agent and person. I've known Jorge for over 10 years and he is the one I turn to whenever my friends or I need assistance with any commercial real estate matters. I know Jorge to be an upstanding businessman, an honorable friend, and an amazing family man and I am proud to consider him my go-to person on commercial real estate."

Vanessa Vasquez de Lara, Esq., Vasquez de Lara Law Group.

"It is no surprise that Mr. Morales' extensive market knowledge in the brokerage community of commercial real estate has led him to produce this impressive work which highlights the truths of the intricate Lease negotiation process. With many years of experience and insights on both Landlord and Tenant representation, this manuscript simplifies for the consumer of real estate product {or Tenant} what you need to know to get a fair deal in a Landlord dominated market."

Jessica Samo, Tishman Speyer

"As a residential real estate broker since 1994, and an entrepreneur with more than 14 leased spaces; never have come across such a knowledgeable commercial real estate expect. Jorge is a force, a calm one. I trust his advices, I trust his expertise and I trust his instincts.

I hope you pick up a copy of his book and set yourself on a path of more success."

Jhonson Napoleon, President, Azure College

DON'T SIGN THE LEASE!

The Tale of a Triumphant Business Owner

Jorge L. Morales

To my wife, my best friend, my love, Diana.

Contents

Preface. ix
Acknowledgements. xiii
Introduction xv

PART ONE
Ten Common Questions

1. What's the Difference between Class A and Class B? 1
2. Do I Pay Rent on Usable or Rentable Square Feet?. 13
3. Parking Ratio – Where Do My Employees Park?. 21
4. Full Service or NNN Lease – What's Included in the Rent? . . . 29
5. When Should I Start Looking for Space?. 43
6. Does TI Stand for Too Much Information? 51
7. LOI Versus RFP – I'm RTG so Can You Explain? 63
8. Do I Need an Option to Renew? 73
9. Is a ROFO Dog Speak? 83
10. My Lease Has Radon Gas?. 93
Part One Conclusion: Mike Johnson Signs a New Lease 99

PART TWO
Avoiding Pitfalls

11. Pitfall One – The Uncooperative Landlord. 107
12. Pitfall Two - Never Sign a Personal Guarantee 115
13. Pitfall Three - Not Possessing a Termination Option 119
14. Pitfall Four - Neglecting Early Access. 125
15. Pitfall Five - The Standard Sublease and Assignment Provision. . .131
16. Pitfall Six - The Relocation Clause 137
17. Pitfall Seven - Hours of Operation – Overtime Charge 141

Epilog - Closing Remarks 149
Appendix A: Class A Property and
             Class B Property Characteristics 151
Appendix B: Common Area Calculations 153
Appendix C:How to Calculate a Parking Ratio 155
Glossary. 157

Preface

In real estate transactions, there are winners, and there are losers. Far too often, the tenant (the business owner) is the loser. Let me explain.

Consider a typical landlord. Rarely will a property owner possess only one building. Even a local or regional owner will own several commercial buildings. Large, national owners such as REITs (Real Estate Investment Trusts), insurance pension funds, and private equity institutions own millions of square feet throughout the United States, and perhaps the world. I once represented a privately held institution that owned more product in New York alone than all the Class A space in downtown Miami and Brickell Avenue markets combined!

Why do I bring this up? Because landlords, whether local, regional, or national, have both intellectual and financial capital on their side, providing them a tremendous advantage. Landlords have a large staff of real estate professionals and years of experience operating their real estate, and rightfully so. The best landlords understand the necessity of employing real estate experts to manage and maintain their properties.

At a minimum, a landlord will employ either directly or indirectly many real estate professionals including property managers, operation directors, chief engineers, maintenance staff, property accountants, asset managers, acquisition directors, real estate attorneys, security guards, general contractors, architects, tenant coordinators, janitorial staff, fire and life safety professionals, landscapers, etc. Obviously, the more properties a landlord owns, the larger the staff which can reach into the thousands for national landlords. Each of these professionals has a unique role I could describe them in detail, but collectively they provide the landlord the knowledge and expertise to apprehend all the ins and outs of leasing and operating their property. For instance, the attorneys have carefully crafted the lease document with one intent: to protect the landlord under any and every conceivable circumstance.

Let's now bring this back to the key point. I have failed to mention one additional expert that nearly every landlord employs. Despite the many real estate professionals working on the landlord's behalf, isn't it amazing that landlords still consider it indispensable to hire a real estate broker to represent their leasing efforts, the leasing agent?

No wonder business owners are at such a disadvantage when they show up to tour space and resolve to negotiate a lease on their own; or use a family friend with a real estate license. Business owners are going up against a highly experienced and well-funded group of professionals who spend their careers in real estate, all working together to get the landlord the best deal possible.

Why did I endeavor to write this book? Because over the course of my career, I've seen many good and well-established companies completely expose themselves to future liabilities and problems, or needlessly leave dollars and beneficial provisions on the table (thereby hampering their business) because they signed a lease highly favorable to the landlord. I have witnessed too many business owners commit many mistakes and fall into dangerous pitfalls found in most standard lease documents— mistakes and pitfalls which all could have easily been avoided.

Don't Sign the Lease! The Tale of a Triumphant Business Owner was written for business owners and decision makers to help protect your interest and negotiate more equitable deals. I want to offer a valuable aide to equip the many business owners who will, sooner or later, need a basic understanding of the inner workings of commercial real estate before engaging in discussions with a landlord and signing a lease.

Business owners shouldn't approach the lease process the way I approach the maintenance of my car. I simply change the oil as I am told and rotate the tires on schedule. But occasionally, I have to spend several hundreds or even thousands of dollars on car repairs at the recommendation of a mechanic. Because I don't know a thing about cars, carburetors, fuel injection, wheel bearings, etc., I simply grin and bear and pay for the repairs placing blind trust in the mechanic. Signing a lease shouldn't be handled in the same fashion. A bad lease will impact a business owner far worse than any costly car repair.

Some in the commercial real estate industry will question, "Why give away trade secrets and behind the scenes information? Why not withhold that knowledge and expertise until you are engaged?" While I understand this thought, I am following the biblical principle that it is more blessed to give than to receive (Acts 20:35). I want to help as many business owners as I can, and this format allows me to reach more business owners than I can possibly represent or assist.

Don't Sign the Lease! The Tale of a Triumphant Business Owner was written to educate, entertain, and transform, based on real life questions and answers, experience, and scenarios (names have been altered of course). Enjoy the reading!

Acknowledgements

To my best friend, helpmeet, heir in grace, supporter, and greatest fan, my wife, Diana—thank you. You have sacrificed much for our family and have listened to all my real estate stories for over twenty years. I love you, darling. To my children, Kayla, Aliana, and Carlos. You bring much joy and pleasure to your father—I love being your dad. I look forward to seeing what God has planned for you. To my parents—thank you for your unconditional love and prayers. To my siblings, Michael and Betty—I'm thankful to have you in my life and love your families.

To Paul L. White, the mentor providentially used to lasso me into a commercial real estate career—thank you. To the Shepherd boys, Brad, Barry, and Brent—we had a great time working together on Brickell Avenue. Those were memorable days. To Jeff Sharmat—we seem to source up business with every discussion. Thank you for your insight and encouragement.

To the many real estate professionals and asset managers who've influenced my career and advanced my knowledge and appreciation of commercial real estate—I thank you. To the numerous clients whom I've had the pleasure of representing: thank you for your trust and confidence. I'm here to serve you.

To the many who have read through the manuscript in its earliest form and have provided valuable input—I am grateful. A special thanks to Mark Schermeister—your offers of help, encouragement, edits, and input were overwhelming displays of kindness.

To Tom Woods—thank you for sparking an entrepreneurial mindset through your podcast that inspired the writing of this book.

All illustrations were done by "Whiteboard Girl." She's the best illustrator on the web.

Editing by Pam Lagomarsino of Above the Pages (www.abovethepages.com) - her talents and skill were a tremendous blessing.

"To the King of the ages, immortal, invisible, the only God, be honor and glory forever and ever. Amen."

Introduction

Meet Michael Johnson: computer expert and video gamer extraordinaire. His friends call him Mike. Mike's parents always desired the best for their son, though they didn't have the means to put him in the best schools. His father could trace their family tree to the pre-American Revolution, and his mother was a second-generation American of Hispanic descent. Mike grew up in a loving home with trips to Grandma's house on Sundays after church. The middle child of three siblings, his father was a conservative Republican and blue-collar worker having spent over thirty years at the same company. His mother was a school teacher (Mike's third-grade teacher) and a concerned Democrat, so Mike learned to charter his course. When he was young, Mike spent far too many hours with his friends around his video game console, though it never impacted his grades. He was a model student.

Mike turned his passion and hobby into a college scholarship and an internship at a local tech company (there's hope parents). He graduated college at the top of his class in under three years with a double major in computer science and software engineering. His dedication to his studies and talent set him apart, and he quickly received job offers from several software companies. Mike accepted a starting position at a new start-up tech company that seemed to fit his enthusiasm and growth potential.

Good decision. Within a few years, Mike was promoted to Software

Engineer revolutionizing the company's software development division. He had a boisterous, outgoing, and positive disposition; he was a natural leader. He quickly advanced to the head of the software engineering division which saw profits soar 20 percent per year since Mike started a few years earlier. Other larger tech companies noted his successes.

An executive recruiter reached out to Mike with an unbelievable opportunity for a director position at a leading software development company. The interview couldn't have gone any better, and the company hired him on the spot. Director of Software Engineering at the software company was Mike's dream job, and at age twenty-seven with a six-figure salary and stock options, he was well on his way to climbing the corporate ladder. His division quickly expanded and dominated its share of the company's profits.

By the end of his third year at the software company, Mike was offered the recently vacated position of company president. At age thirty and recently married, he was in charge of one of the fastest growing and trendiest software companies in his hometown. Mike left his ordinary cube and moved to the coveted corner office. Through the glass walls, he could observe the many code programmers and engineers which worked in cohesive groups and was available to all the teams.

After a grueling prep meeting for a presentation to the board the next week, Mike returned to his office. Sitting down at his desk, Mike grabbed a notepad to review the to-do list he had jotted down earlier that morning. "*Not too much progress,*" he thought. As he was bemoaning the thought of another day with unfinished business, he noticed a blinking red light on his phone indicating he had a voice message. In fact, he had five voice messages:

- Message one: "Mr. Johnson, congratulations on your promotion. I am Kasey with a national real estate company. You've probably noticed our signs everywhere. I'm calling about your pending lease expiration. I'd like to come by your office for a brief meeting to discuss the market and how great we are. Please call me."

- Message two: "Michael, hello. I'm "Lucky" Tom, a tenant representative for a global real estate group. Our integrated platform is huge. We even have offices in China. As your lease expires in twelve months, I'd like to pitch for your business. Together we can make your company great again. We have lots of pretty charts and flyers. Trust me; they're fantastic. Call me."

- Message three: "Mr. Johnson, my name is Ms. Carter, and I work with a tenant representation company. We only represent tenants such as yourself and no landlords. We have no conflicts, nope, not one, nada—we are not conflicted. Your lease is set to expire soon, and I'd like to show you all the subleases I have in the market. Did I mention, we have no conflicts? None. Please call me."

- Message four: "Michael, I am Bob, the Closer, of Bob the Closer Real Estate Company, and the President of Bob the Closer Real Estate Company. I can save you money. Your landlord is charging thirty dollars per square foot, but I can get you a twenty dollar rate and a hefty TI package. Call me now to save your job. Bob, the Closer of Bob the Closer Real Estate Company, and uh, I am the principal."

- Message five: "Mr. Johnston, I am Jason Woods with a local real estate company. I recently represented a tenant in your property and would tell you all about the deal, but I signed a confidentiality agreement, so I can't. I can help you with your lease expiration. Please call me at your convenience."

Well, at least four of the five got my name right, thought Mike. As he finished listening to the five messages, he noticed another call came in that went straight to voice mail.

- Message six: "Listen, Michael, what's the matter? Don't you want to save money on your lease? It's Bob, the Closer of Bob the Closer Real Estate Company, and it's been one hour since I left you a message. I will call you every hour of each day until you call me back. Don't be a loser, call me back."

Mike bombarded by brokers

What is going on? Who are these people, and how do they know my lease expires in twelve months? I don't even know when my lease expires, wondered Mike placing the phone down and hoping for no more calls.

Unfortunately, after much diligence, Mike confirmed the software company's full floor lease does expire in twelve months. Much to his aggravation, brokers, especially Bob, the Closer, continued to pepper him with daily calls looking for business. The constant solicitations kept the lease expiration at the forefront of Mike's mind. *What am I going to do about the lease?*

One week later, the leasing agent for the landlord of the property, Tony Di Proprietario, invited Mike out to lunch and Mike accepted. After the customary congratulatory comments and small talk, Tony put him on the spot. Taking his notepad that had been resting on the corner of the table covered with a white tablecloth, the leasing agent smiled in between bites of his salad, "So, now that the lease is set to run out within twelve months, have you given any thought to your renewal?"

"Before you answer, let me tell you about all the planned improvements at the property," continued Tony. "As you know, the building sold recently, and the new landlord is investing a lot of money in renovations which will transform our property from a Class B building to a Class A building." As the waiter refreshed their water, Tony explained, in tremendous detail, how new marble floors in the lobby, the planned conference center, and gym facility would all increase the value of the property.

"Wow, that's uh, that's—that's well and good," interjected Mike, as he buttered a piece of bread. He was noticeably uncomfortable with the discussion not really sure what a Class B or Class A building meant.

Tony didn't pick up on Mike's body language but zeroed in on Mike's words, "well and good."

"Do you still need the same rentable square feet or will you need more space—which is okay, because we have an excellent common area factor and our parking ratio can handle any expansion," continued Tony.

"We are also considering switching from a full-service lease to an NNN lease. But don't worry, we'll make sure the operating expenses stay relatively the same as your base year."

At this point, all Mike could muster was a simple nod as he tried to make sense of the dialogue and enjoy his pasta dish that had finally arrived.

Tony was on a roll. "I have a lot of activity on the vacant spaces in the building, and I'm about ready to forward you a ROFO Notice on the available space below your office. Oh, could you pass the salt please?" The last request was about all Mike understood, and he quickly obliged.

Tony proceeded, "Thanks. So, you can appreciate the landlord would like to know if you plan on exercising your option to renew, the notice is due next month. Keep in mind if you need TI we're happy to accommodate although your option language doesn't include a TIA."

Tony suddenly and awkwardly leaned forward, looked around the restaurant, and whispered, "I'll be sure to get you a good deal" as his tie nearly landed on Mike's meatball.

Mike wished he had a translator to explain the foreign language the leasing agent appeared to be speaking. *Class A, rentable square feet, common area factor, parking ratio, full-service, NNN, base year, ROFO Notice, TI, TIA, option to renew, etc. What did this all signify?* Mike stopped eating with half the pasta still on his dish (and a meatball); somehow, he had lost his appetite. He commented to the leasing agent, "All good questions to consider, Tony." He then answered the way many decision makers answer when caught off guard; he appealed to a higher authority: "I'll need to speak to my executive committee and report back to you."

"No problem," responded the leasing agent as he pored over the dessert menu, "I'll prepare an LOI for your review, and I am happy to send it to your tenant advisor. Who is your tenant advisor?" asked Tony as the waiter approached the table to remove the lunch plates.

"Would you care for some coffee?" asked the waiter.

Just then, Mike's cell phone rang. *At last, a break in this tiresome discourse,* he thought. "Excuse me; I must take this call."

Grabbing his cell phone, he stepped outside the restaurant, and answered the call, "Hi, this is Mike Johnson."

"Fantastic. Mike, this is the best day of your life. It's Bob, the Closer, of Bob the Closer Real Estate Company."

Have you ever been in Mike's shoes? Have you ever been Bob the *closered* by real estate agents cold calling you daily for business? Has a Tony, the leasing agent, at any point pressed you for a renewal? Mike's story is quite common.

If you own a business or are a decision maker, regardless of the size of your company, you will eventually sign a commercial lease (if you haven't already). Rent is often the second highest expense for the business community, second only to payroll. But just as a good employee contributes mightily to the profitability of a firm, a well-negotiated lease will likewise promote the company's values, morale, and profit margins.

Don't Sign the Lease! The Tale of a Triumphant Business Owner is comprised of two parts. In part one, we explore the journey of Mike Johnson, a fictional businessman who is a typical "OBO," an Overwhelmed Business Owner, and follow his transformation to a "TBO," a Triumphant Business Owner. I'll define these terms shortly. In Mike's story, we'll answer ten common questions every business owner must know and understand before signing a lease document. In part two, we'll discover seven frequent mistakes business owners commit regarding lease agreements and how to avoid these costly mistakes. I've spent much time in my career representing landlords as a leasing agent. I've been behind the curtain. I know how they think, what drives them, what's important to them, and most importantly, the errors tenants unknowingly make when signing a lease.

Consider this: most Fortune 500 companies triumphantly sign a tenant-favorable lease. Why? These large institutions employ directors of real estate to negotiate their leases across many markets. These in-house directors possess real estate degrees, many obtaining Master's Degrees in real estate and additional certifications, making them experts in commercial real estate. Yet, these same real estate directors engage the services of tenant advisors in each local market where their corporation signs a lease.

Fortune 500 companies apprehend the indispensable advantage and value of understanding each local market nuance and lease provision – bestowing on them the title of TBO—Triumphant Business Owner. Still, many business owners go about the lease process on their own. Too frequently business owners blindly sign the lease provided directly by the landlord thereby causing irreparable injury to their business leading to an inevitable OBO—Overwhelmed Business Owner.

Overwhelmed Business Owners—OBO

- ➢ Leave their field of expertise and branch out to find space on their own
- ➢ Begrudgingly and timidly sign a lease
- ➢ Don't fully understand and comprehend the lease document
- ➢ Expose themselves and their businesses to future liabilities
- ➢ Control of their space is in the landlord's possession
- ➢ Sign a document that protects the landlord's best interest
- ➢ Overlook the importance of market trends and opportunities
- ➢ Think they have a good deal from the landlord
- ➢ Often surprised by notices and rent statements by the landlord
- ➢ Overwhelmed by a landlord favorable lease throughout the term

Triumphant Business Owners—TBO

- ➢ Leverage the services, expertise, and knowledge of tenant advisors
- ➢ Confidently and boldly sign a lease
- ➢ Have a firm understanding and comprehension of the lease document
- ➢ Safeguard themselves and their business from future liabilities
- ➢ Control of the space is in their possession
- ➢ Sign a document that protects their best interest
- ➢ Become market experts apprehending the trends and opportunities
- ➢ Quantifiably can prove they have a good deal compared to the market
- ➢ Well prepared for landlord notices and rent statements
- ➢ Triumphantly enjoy a tenant-favorable lease throughout the term

> **OBOs sign lease documents. TBOs sign opportune vehicles leading to the success and growth of their business ventures**

OBOs sign lease documents. TBOs sign opportune vehicles leading to the success and growth of their business ventures.

Don't sign the lease! At least not until you can sign as a Triumphant Business Owner. My prayer for this book is that it will provide many business owners the essential knowledge and tools to become Triumphant Business Owners.

How about Mike Johnson? Will Mike approach his lease expiration, to borrow an illustration from a friend, like a blindfolded man on a pogo stick hopping through a mine field? Will he negotiate a deal directly against the well-capitalized landlord and Tony the veteran leasing agent? Will he endeavor to tour alternate properties and sign a lease on his own? Or will he seek professional guidance? Mike is an Overwhelmed Business Owner. Well, let's seek to help Mike Johnson become a Triumphant Business Owner.

I hope you will find this book informative, profitable, and perhaps a little entertaining. I created all characters, names, events, dialogue, and details for fictionalization as a reference for real business practices.

PART ONE

Ten Common Questions

Triumphant
Having won a battle or contest; victorious

1

What's the Difference between Class A and Class B?

Let's take a look at Mike Johnson's situation. Having been recently promoted to president, Mike is responsible for the office lease which expires within twelve months—this wasn't explained to him when he accepted the promotion. The full floor lease currently costs the company hundreds of thousands of dollars annually. The leasing agent for the property is a seasoned commercial real estate broker with decades of experience representing landlords. The landlord, having recently purchased the property, is a publicly traded REIT (Real Estate Investment Trust) that owns over twenty million square feet throughout the U.S. and self-performs the management of the property.

Mike's supersonic rise to president of the software company already earned him the credentials of being an up-and-coming executive in the software development world. Even though a software genius, he doesn't have a degree in real estate or a real estate license. He has never searched for office space or signed a lease. Mike hasn't even read his lease. And now he oversees real estate decisions which will contractually bind the software company to millions of dollars in a lease agreement.

Mike will also need to tackle this added workload while attending Lamaze classes as he recently learned his wife is expecting their first child. Further raising the high stakes, a colleague at the company informed Mike to watch his back since a few board members of the software company (led by Mr. Curmudgeon) questioned if he was ready for the role as president. All corporate eyes would be meticulously watching Mike during this transition.

Mike Johnson decided wisely the best route for his pending lease expiration was to get the assistance of a tenant advisor to represent his real estate interest. The lunch conversation with Tony, the leasing agent, was all the convincing he needed to seek help from a commercial real estate professional. Besides, it seemed Tony expected Mike to have representation. Mike called back and interviewed the five commercial real estate brokers who had left him messages. After meeting with all five, he engaged Jason Woods of a local real estate company to represent the software company.

Woods was a twenty-year-plus commercial real estate broker, who had just left a national firm to form his local real estate company. He had spent a significant portion of his career representing landlords and brought a different, behind-the-curtain perspective to the tenant advisor role than the other brokers did. Jason was one of the few brokers who appeared to be truly interested in Mike's plight and not just a commission—Mike and Jason connected early. Jason also had a firm understanding of the market and a grasp of the process toward a successful lease signing.

> **But how much is this going to cost me? Nothing Michael.**

Before officially retaining Jason as his tenant advisor, Mike had a pressing question: "Okay, I'm convinced I need the services of a tenant advisor. But how much is this going to cost me?"

"Nothing Michael. The landlord pays the tenant advisory fees when all parties sign a lease," answered Jason. "Our agreement will even state I will look only to the property owner for my payment."

"But won't I get a better deal if the landlord saves that money? Oh, and please call me Mike."

"Landlords budget for the brokerage commissions of the landlord broker and tenant advisor for each deal. In a typical listing agreement, if a tenant negotiates on his own, the landlord's broker makes a higher fee, perhaps double—so if there are any savings, it's minimal," answered Jason. "In my years representing landlords, I can affirm that landlords understand the collaborative efforts of a tenant advisor play an integral part in preserving the integrity of the leasing process providing for smoother transactions."

"I didn't follow that last line," said Mike who wasn't afraid to voice his thoughts.

"It's easier to get a deal done with a tenant advisor at hand."

Mike signed the tenant representation agreement assigning Jason Woods as the software company's exclusive tenant advisor. Jason quickly went to work. He spent time with Mike listening to his objectives and goals for the office and abstracted his current lease. A lease abstract summarizes all the business points and key provisions of the lease in a brief and orderly form.

Shortly after Mike signed the tenant representation agreement, the two met at Mike's office for a kick-off session. Jason Woods prepared the software company kick-off checklist to serve as the agenda for the meeting. The kick-off checklist provided the order and course of action for Mike all the way to the lease signing and commencement of the lease.

Market Overview

The first item on the kick-off checklist was a thorough review of the current office-market conditions. The market review including current vacancies (space available for lease), rental rates (per square foot), absorption (a measurement of the space leased over a specific time), comparables (comparisons between properties), new and planned construction, and trends equipped Mike to be a well-informed participant in his software company's search for a new corporate address.

"I didn't realize rental rates were that high," Mike said.

"Yes, the market has definitely recovered the last few years," Jason replied. "We haven't seen any new construction in five years—therefore tenant demand is absorbing vacancy rapidly."

Jason divided the market presentation into Class A and Class B properties which naturally paved the way to the next item on the checklist: questions and answers of common commercial real estate terminology. In their discussions, he briefed Mike on the differences between Class A and Class B properties.

Class A and Class B

Tony, the leasing agent, in Mike's building, highlighted the property was transforming from Class B to Class A. Brokers are quick to ask, "Do you prefer Class A or Class B?" providing no context to the question. Some would like to answer, "I finished school—no Class A or Class B for me, thank you." You know, I'm not speaking about a class with a professor and students, but rather a classification of properties.

"How are properties classified as Class A or Class B?" Mike asked.

"In answering the question, Mike, let's first rule out what is not intended when we say a property is Class A or Class B," said Jason. "First, a Class B property is not necessarily a lower-class property than a Class A one. A property designated as Class B may be maintained and managed in the same first-class manner as a Class A property."

"That's true. I'm pleased with the current property condition which Tony, the leasing agent, identified as Class B."

"You should expect many of the same services in either scenario. Similarly, a Class B building may be in the same or a better neighborhood than a Class A building. It's not an insult to lease space in a Class B building rather than a Class A building. This is not class warfare," Jason said.

"Second, a Class A property is not necessarily larger than a Class B property. Class B properties may be larger than Class A properties and vice versa; size does not automatically classify a property," explained

Jason who wanted to be sure his new client had a firm understanding of what defines Class A and B properties.

"What about small buildings such as the corner drug store?"

"Good catch," said Jason. "Small-sized properties, such as a free-standing bank branch or any other single purpose building, do not fit into our discussion of property classes."

Class A and Class B?

DON'T SIGN THE LEASE!

"Are Class A properties newer than Class B properties?" asked Mike. "I definitely don't want to lease space in a property older than I am."

As Mike asked the question, an employee of the software company peered into the office and informed Mike he had a call, "Mike, there's a Bob, the Closer on the line. He said he's the president of Bob the Closer Real Estate Company and your *close* friend."

"I can assure you he's not my close friend," said Mike shaking his head. "Could you please forward the call to voice mail? Thanks." Mike looked at Jason as though helpless. Jason smiled and continued with Mike's question.

"Class A properties are not always newer than Class B properties," answered Jason. "Sure, a newly constructed property will be considered Class A. But there are many older properties—some twenty, thirty, or forty-year-old recently updated buildings, so they continue to hold their Class A status. At the same time, primarily in the suburban markets, some newly constructed properties were built in a fashion that designates them as Class B."

> **The answer, in one word, is value**

"What then *is* the difference between a Class A and a Class B building?"

"The answer, in one word, is value," said Jason. "Value is often a subjective judgment of the one surveying the possibilities."

"To one, a Hyundai automobile delivers solid, reliable, and consistent value. To another, a Tesla offers a tremendous value for a luxury sports car. Both vehicles feature air conditioning, AM/FM radio, cruise control, and leather seats. Both cars will take you to your destination, but one has a much higher sticker price. Although the Tesla may be priced up to $50,000 more than the Hyundai and offers more bells and whistles, car salespeople can say both cars offer their owners good value."

7

"I'm glad you used my car in the example," said Mike with a grin. "I'll let you guess which one I drive."

"Property classifications can be described in the same way," said Jason. "The value of a Class A property compared to a Class B depends primarily on the needs, purpose, and clientele of each business. Does your business need nine-foot ceilings or eight-foot ceilings? Is it vital to your business, employees, and visitors to have valet service? Would you and your employees make use of a conference center or gym facilities? Does your business presence depend on a grand lobby entrance?"

"Then a Class A property features more bells and whistles than a Class B property?"

"Exactly, right on!" answered an enthusiastic Jason.

"I can picture my employees using the gym facilities and making use of a conference center for our monthly research and development meetings."

"We'll need to note that as we search for alternate office locations; it sounds like a Class A property might be the right fit for your firm," said Jason.

"And I value the higher ceilings in the office. That's a must on our wish list too," said Mike.

"One easily identifiable feature differentiating Class A from Class B is finished ceiling heights. In our market, a property cannot be designated Class A without nine-foot ceilings," responded Jason taking notes of their conversation.

"Can't all properties accommodate high ceilings?" inquired Mike.

"Not all properties. Some older properties were designed with lower finished ceilings in mind."

"I assume then that new buildings are constructed to provide nine-foot ceilings," said Mike.

"Usually yes, but not always," said Jason who then enlightened Mike with the following story:

A residential developer ventured into the commercial realm to develop an office building in a highly sought-after submarket. After two years, the developer finally received a Certificate of Occupancy or the "CO," the final municipal approval declaring the property complete and ready for occupancy. Potential tenants were eager to tour the newly constructed office tower in a submarket that had not seen a new product in over ten years. New marble floors in the grand lobby welcomed visitors, and a beautifully designed elevator took prospects up to the office floors. Each floor was in "raw condition" meaning unimproved and open with nothing but concrete floors and a concrete ceiling. The expansive window line built to current construction codes featured beautiful city and ocean views. Everything seemed perfect at the new office tower.

A law firm, led by Partner Smith, signed a ten-year lease for a full floor. The law firm agreed to the market rental rates for the new Class A office building. Six months later the developer completed the tenant improvements and tendered possession of the premises to Mr. Smith's law firm.

To the shock of Mr. Smith, when they moved in, the ceilings seemed very low and not what they expected from a new Class A property. Certainly, competitively priced properties offered at least nine-foot ceilings, but this new space didn't seem to be anywhere near that height. Taking a tape measure and balancing himself on an office chair that swiveled with every breath, the business owner measured the finished ceiling height at eight feet and four inches, which is more in line with a

Class B property—not a pricey Class A property. "What happened?" questioned Mr. Smith. "Maybe it's just my office." He had the other attorneys measure the ceiling heights in their offices. "All the offices measure eight feet and four inches," reported the office clerk who had gathered the surveys from the attorneys.

"This can't be right," said Mr. Smith.

Had Mr. Smith (or a tenant advisor representing Mr. Smith) asked the developer during the tour, "What is the slab-to-slab height?" He would have realized a ten-foot six-inch height would never be capable of delivering a Class A ceiling. Likewise, had the developer obtained guidance from an expert commercial real estate advisor, the property would have been built with enough clearance for Class A ceilings. It turned out that once the market became aware of the lower finished ceilings, tenants were no longer willing to pay premium rental rates for the new building."

"Sounds like the law firm should have hired you, Jason."

"We tried, but the managing partner wanted to go about the process on his own," commented Jason with a bit of disappointment he couldn't help the overwhelmed business owner. "For many companies, ceiling heights are non-impactful to the use and productivity of the office. However, in Mr. Smith's case, he willfully signed a lengthy lease at higher rates expecting a Class A property which now featured a Class B finished ceiling height."

"What are other Class A property features?"

Property Features

"There are many features: onsite security guard service, covered parking, ground floor restaurants, and amenities such as conference centers and gym facilities," answered Jason. "These features cost more to construct and manage, and are stereotypically found in higher rent properties such as Class A buildings."

"The leasing agent, Tony Di Proprietario, mentioned my current landlord was planning on spending substantial capital upgrading the Class B building into a Class A building adding marble floors, a gym, and a conference center," remarked Mike. "Tony said the renovations 'would increase the value of the property.' Uh, what did he mean by that?" asked a skeptical Mike.

"I believe the leasing agent gave you a critical hint to expect an increase in the base rent due to the renovations," said Jason. "He might of well have said, 'Mike, we plan on charging you a much higher rental rate than you are currently paying for your renewal to make up for dollars the landlord is spending on the renovations,'" finished Jason.

"Why is that?" asked Mike.

"Broadly speaking, Class A properties will demand higher rental rates than Class B properties. However, this may not always be the case as certain outliers can frequently exist," responded Jason. Along these lines, Jason described a prime downtown market, where Class B office product located on a bustling boardwalk will out-perform, by way of occupancy and rates, Class A space elsewhere in the downtown market. The overwhelming benefit of being located on the boardwalk including the constant tourist influx and local traffic, and the many restaurants and shops, overshadows and diminishes any differences between Class A and Class B.

"The real difference between Class A and Class B is what a business owner is willing to pay for the perceived value of the varying property features in each respective market," stated Jason concluding the conversation. "Is covered parking valuable enough to a tenant that they will pay 20 percent more in base rent? Is the difference between ownership groups or ocean views enough to warrant paying the equivalent of an additional year of rent over a five-year lease term?"

For Mike Johnson, an on-site gym facility would be a great benefit to his programmers and engineers who could use respites and breaks throughout their grueling day. The higher ceilings were a must, and a conference center would save the software company square footage. Based on their initial kick-off discussion, Jason Woods and Mike Johnson resolved the list of possible office locations would only include Class A properties.

In summary, each market chooses the property attributes that will classify buildings as a Class A or Class B property. (Please refer to Appendix A for a fuller list of Class A features as compared to Class B).

"All that to say, Mike is that you, the business owner will ultimately determine the eventual monetary worth of a Class A property or Class B property. How about that?"

As the kick-off meeting continued, Jason informed Mike that one of the next steps for the software company entailed deciding the ideal size for the office today and over the next five years. The discussion naturally progressed into another question from Mike to his tenant advisor regarding square footage.

2

Do I Pay Rent on Usable or Rentable Square Feet?

Business owners, including Mike Johnson, are sometimes shocked to find out the landlord is charging them for more space than they occupy. When the proposal or lease states the premises or space is fifteen thousand *rentable* square feet, tenants often assume they will *occupy* fifteen thousand square feet. The rent will be calculated on the fifteen thousand square feet.

"What am I paying for?"

"The truth is the actual measurement of the space is often 15–20 percent less than the square footage a tenant pays for as defined in the lease," commented Jason Woods as he and Mike continued the question and answer portion of the kick-off meeting. "Many business owners realize this only after a lease is signed. Many times, it's the tenant's furniture vendor or space planner, hired to dress the space with furniture, fixtures, or equipment who brings this to their attention."

"You mean the actual measurement of my office doesn't add up to fifteen thousand square feet?" asked a puzzled Mike.

"That's right," affirmed Jason and he continued the discussion with the accompanying story.

A business owner decided to move into a larger office in a suburban office park setting. The leasing agent at the

13

preferred location insisted on a ten-year term (the term is the length of the lease). To the business owner, the ten-year lease seemed an exhaustive commitment, but he was offered a better rental rate in exchange for a ten-year term (versus the five-year term he initially desired). A few days after touring the property, the business owner signed the lease at the urgent prompting of the leasing agent who was eager to close a deal.

Thirty days later, the landlord's property manager notified the business owner that the space was freshly painted and carpeted and ready to be occupied. As this was a new office, the business owner planned on ordering new office furniture. He visited the premises a week before the planned move to take measurements of the offices to be sure the new desks and credenzas would fit.

Armed with the space plan, the business owner began the tedious task of taking a tape measure to every office.

The business owner measures his office

After a few hours, the business owner had measured every square inch of the office space, and for curiosity sake, he totaled the measurements. "Why am I coming up short on the total square footage?" He tallied the measurements a second and third time, and he continued to arrive at a lower number than the square footage in the lease. The business owner was beyond agitated and felt ripped off by the landlord. "I can't fit all my accountants in this space!" Monday morning could not come too soon.

By 8:30 a.m. Monday morning, an irate business owner greeted the leasing agent at the landlord's office, "You cheated me! You leased me twenty-five hundred square feet, and the space only measures two thousand square feet. I want my lease adjusted, or I'm not moving in!"

"Oh, did you calculate the usable square footage or the rentable square footage?" the leasing agent quickly asked.

"Usable or rentable square footage, what's the difference?" asked the business owner.

Jason concluded the story by stating, "A business owner may believe he was taken advantage of if the landlord or leasing agent did not explicitly explain the difference between usable and rentable square feet."

"I can understand his displeasure."

"This could be avoided with clarifications up front during a tour by an experienced tenant advisor or leasing agent," retorted Jason. "One of my worst days in commercial real estate came early in my career as a leasing agent when I failed to inform a start-up business owner of the difference between usable and rentable square feet. After measuring his space over the weekend, the angry business owner visited me on a Monday morning and called me several names which I cannot repeat. Lesson learned."

Usable and Rentable Square Feet

"What *is* the difference between usable square feet and rentable square feet?"

"Usable square foot (USF for short) is the space a tenant occupies," answered Jason. "To keep it simple, if you were to measure the space, the usable square footage would be calculated. Even this calculation is subjective, and depending on what industry standard is used, the tape measure would have to go to the outside wall or windows and measure a few inches into each demising wall (the walls that separate the space from other tenants and common area hallways). Generally speaking, your tape measurement is the usable square feet. This is the true measurement of the occupied space."

> **Generally speaking, your tape measurement is the usable square feet.**

"So how do landlords come up with a larger square foot number?"

"The greater square footage number is known as rentable square feet (RSF for short)," replied Jason. "Industry organizations such as BOMA International, which stands for Building Owners and Managers Association International, delineate standards by which property owners can increase the usable square feet or occupant space. The larger square footage incorporates the proportionate share of the common areas of the occupied floor and building which benefit the occupant of the space."

Jason then looked up BOMA International's website on his laptop which has been resting on the edge of Mike's desk. Turning the laptop to face Mike, he said, "The following is an excerpt from BOMA International's website (www.boma.org):

'This latest version, Office Buildings: Standard Methods of Measurement (ANSI/BOMA Z65.1 – 2010), provides a uniform basis for measuring rentable area in both existing and new office buildings by taking a building-wide approach to floor area measurement. It provides a methodology for measuring both occupant space as well as the space that benefits all occupants.'"

"What's space that benefits all occupants?" asked Mike intently looking at the laptop still reading through the different headings.

"Space that benefits building occupants can include the restrooms, ground floor lobby, elevator lobby landings, and hallways on the floor leading to the occupant spaces," answered Jason. "A percentage share of the first-floor lobby and additional amenities such as a gym, conference facilities, or the building's staff offices may or may not be included. All the building areas located outside the occupant space, except vertical penetrations (such as exit stairways), can be referred to as common areas."

"I recall Tony, the leasing agent, mentioning the phrase common area factor. Does that have to do with usable versus rentable square footage?"

"Yes, it does," confirmed Jason. "The sum of the common areas within a property that benefit the occupant of the usable area are proportionately calculated per floor, and a common area factor is derived. A common area factor (also called an add-on factor), which can vary between 15–20 percent for multi-tenant floors (and sometimes higher), is then added on to the usable square footage to calculate the rentable square feet. There is a host of methods landlords use to calculate the rentable square footage including loss factor and core factor. Most landlords in our market use a common area factor. This add-on factor accounts for the discrepancy in size between the usable and rentable square footage." (Please refer to Appendix B for common area calculation)

"Let me guess. Landlords charge rent on the higher rentable square footage, not the lower usable square footage?" asked Mike though he already knew the answer.

"Sadly, landlords tabulate rent on the rentable square footage," answered Jason shaking his head. He explained, "Because landlords maintain, air condition, and clean the common areas and pay the real estate taxes and insurance for the common areas, they pass on these costs to each tenant by charging rent on the higher rentable square footage rather than the smaller usable square footage."

"If I follow you, then rentable square footage incorporates the percentage of common areas that benefit the occupied space, while usable square footage measures just the occupied space? Did I get that right?" asked Mike rather impressed with his comprehension of the subject.

"Correct sir. Spot on," affirmed Jason with a high-five, glad to have his client grasp the rentable square foot concept.

"Do all properties use a common area factor?"

"No, not all. Retail and industrial properties which do not customarily feature common areas charge rent only on usable square feet."

"Therefore, when we tour space and the leasing agent states the size of the space, it's important to inquire about the common area factor," stated Mike straightening up on his chair as he experienced an epiphany.

"Imperative!" asserted Jason. "Comparable analysis between properties under consideration must take into account the usable square footage and the common area factor. Only then will you have a true picture of how much your space will cost as well as the rent per employee."

As Mike pondered that last statement, Jason added, "Mike, I believe one of the best metrics for measuring the space affordability is the rent per employee. The common area factor plays a tremendous role in this metric."

"I've never heard of rent per employee. Can you explain this phrase?" asked an interested Mike.

"Sure," answered Jason. "This factor is derived by dividing the monthly or annual base rent by the number of employees that fit into the space. The lower the factor, the better."

"Seems like a logical way to look at your rent cost."

"Even if a space cost slightly more monthly rent than a competitive option, with an efficient common area factor, we may be able to squeeze more employees into the space. The more employees will produce a lower rent per employee factor. For some of my clients in higher education, we look at rent per student," retorted Jason.

"Makes perfect sense. Thanks, Jason."

In our illustration, the business owner with the tape measure would have saved much aggravation if the leasing agent had explained the difference between usable and rentable square feet during the tour. An experienced tenant advisor can guide you through this process to help calculate which property offers you the most cost-effective and efficient option for your business.

Mike anticipated growing from his current thirty programmers and engineers to upward of fifty professionals. He didn't anticipate all fifty employees in the office each day except the monthly research and development meetings. The thought of adding more staff in the office raised another key question for Jason to answer.

3

Parking Ratio — Where Do My Employees Park?

"Where do my employees park?" Mike asked his tenant advisor, Jason Woods, as they continued the question and answer portion of the kick-off meeting.

"What a simple and practical question, yet one often overlooked."

"We can all sympathize with a business owner who finds out too late that his employees cannot find parking when they arrive in the morning or return from lunch," mentioned Jason as he focused on Mike's question. "Or when it rains (which is frequent in many areas), much of the parking is under water and not accessible."

"I hate when that happens."

"During a rainstorm, I once had to take off my socks and shoes and roll my pants up to my knees to get to the office—and my pants still got soaked!" added Jason.

"Did you send the landlord a laundry bill?"

"I should have!" replied Jason. "Locating alternative or additional parking for employees can be time-consuming and costly. Valet parking or stacking cars are poor solutions for employee parking dilemmas."

"Why is that?"

"Both alternatives delay the time it takes for employees to park in the morning, return from lunch or at the end of the day, leave the office."

21

"Yikes! I didn't think of that. I don't want our engineers losing precious working time waiting to park their cars!"

"Even worse is when a customer drives around looking for a parking spot," interjected Jason. "Business owners spend considerable dollars and marketing efforts to drive customers to visit the office for that one brief opportunity to make a presentation. Then the day of the scheduled meeting arrives, and your potential client endures the frustrations of not being able to find a parking space. The visitor either leaves or arrives late and agitated to the presentation. Don't count on closing the sale."

Parking lot full — I'm leaving!

"I can picture the scene. That would be a major problem," confirmed Mike.

> **One of the most impactful property features for your business is parking.**

"One of the most impactful property features for your business is parking. In particular, adequate parking to meet your employee and visitor needs."

"I assumed all properties provided adequate parking," confessed Mike appreciating that Jason was forewarning him of this important matter.

"Sufficient parking will ultimately be one key factor in choosing whether a specific market and property are best suited for your company address," continued Jason. "Establishing if a property can handle your parking requirement should be located near the top of the priority list."

"How do we do this?"

"To make this judgment, I recommend a twofold approach: a common sense inspection and review of the building's parking ratio," answered Jason who added, "First, you should always consider a visual, common sense inspection of the property's parking area, both surface level, and garage parking."

"Is that really necessary? What if the leasing agent states the property can handle your parking needs?"

Common Sense Inspection

"Regardless of what the property claims to offer, the parking areas should pass a simple eye test," retorted Jason. "For example, if you have fifty employees working full day shifts and receive five visitors a day, a full parking lot or only finding twenty empty spots during the tour is a major red flag."

"True, that makes sense."

"Another red flag is when the building's parking areas are more occupied than the actual property," offered Jason.

"What do you mean?"

"If the property is 50 percent leased, but the parking area is at 75 percent capacity, there is room for concern. Perhaps an existing tenant is over parking, or the property has over allocated parking to tenants. Expect parking to be a problem," replied Jason.

"Understood," nodded Mike.

"Another essential common sense inspection revolves around peak parking hours. Should the property tour be conducted during off-peak business hours, a return to the property during normal standard operating conditions would be ideal," added Jason.

"What are off-peak hours?"

"Obvious off-peak hours include holidays and weekends, although these would be extremely rare touring times. Less subtle off-peak times include teacher work days, non-federal holidays such as Jewish holidays, the summer season, the week of Thanksgiving and the last two weeks of the year," answered Jason. He added, "Oh, and early morning (before 9:00 AM), late afternoon (after 5 PM), and lunch time may also not offer a true picture of the property's parking condition."

Jason wrapped up his thoughts on the common sense visual inspection. Mike realized he would have assumed a property could accommodate the software company's parking requirement if it hadn't been for Jason's input. But he still questioned what a parking ratio entailed.

Parking Ratio

"Thanks for that insight, Jason. We can avoid many parking troubles by a common sense visual inspection. But what about this parking ratio I hear so much about? What is that?" asked Mike recalling his lunch conversation with the leasing agent. Tony Di Proprietario assured Mike the building could handle his parking needs if he needed more space because the property had a good parking ratio. "What's a parking ratio?" asked Mike.

Jason was on the same track as his client and was prepared next to discuss parking ratios. "The property's parking ratio is how many parking spaces the landlord will guarantee to the tenant for every one thousand rentable square feet leased," answered Jason. "Typically, the proposal and the lease agreement will include a provision concerning parking. Most landlords will guarantee an amount of parking based on a parking ratio (or at least they should)." He offered this example:

"Property A features a parking ratio of 4:1000 (pronounced four per thousand) while Property B features a parking ratio of 3:1000. The company needing ten thousand rentable square feet would be guaranteed forty parking spaces in Property A's building parking area and thirty parking spaces in Property B's building parking areas."

"How did you maneuver from the parking ratio to the actual number of parking spaces?"

Jason clarified, "To convert the parking ratio to the number of parking spaces, simply divide the total number of rentable square feet being leased by one thousand; and then multiply that figure by the number of parking spaces per one thousand the landlord is offering." (Please refer to the Appendix C for an illustrated chart on calculating the parking ratio).

Jason summarized the discussion by succinctly adding, "If we sign a lease for a ten thousand square foot space at Property A with a parking ratio of 4:1000, we can expect forty employees to park during business hours. Were this not to be the case, the landlord would be in default of the lease."

"So, we'll need to do a thorough visual inspection of the parking areas and obtain the parking ratio. Once we have both, then we can surmise if the property can properly and consistently accommodate our parking needs?" questioned Mike.

"That's it," affirmed Jason.

"Knowing we'll need to cram many employees into our space, where can we find the best parking scenario?" asked an intrigued Mike.

"Historically, greater parking accessibility can be found in the suburban markets while less parking accessibility is expected in the Central Business Districts (CBD)," answered Jason happy to apply his years of experience to the conversation. "Parking ratios in the CBD markets can vary from 1:1000 to 2:1000 whereas parking ratios increase up to 4:1000 to 5:1000 in the suburban markets. Obviously, as a higher density user, the software company should consider submarkets that can accommodate higher parking requirements."

"We've discussed a property's ability to accommodate parking, but what about parking cost?" asked Mike. "At least my current owner doesn't charge for parking."

"Definitely, parking cost is an important consideration which can vary between submarkets," answered Jason. "Traditionally, the CBD markets will charge a monthly fee per parking space which can add up to three to six dollars per square foot per year in additional rent."

"Did you say three to six dollars per square foot in additional rent? Wow! That will never work for the software company," exclaimed Mike shocked that any tenant could pay those fees.

"Yep. That's the case in the CBD markets," reiterated Jason. "Parking is ordinarily free in the suburban markets. A plethora of free parking is one reason the higher density users, such as back office operations and call centers, congregate primarily in the suburban markets while law firms and financial firms assemble in the CBD markets."

"Jason, my company is pleased to be in the suburbs, trust me."

"Mike, in closing our parking discussion, let me offer a few additional constructive considerations which can decrease future parking problems," stated Jason wanting to prepare his client fully. "While valet parking is a desirous Class A amenity in CBD markets, valet parking is abnormal in the suburban markets."

"Really? I thought that was offered as an amenity," responded a surprised Mike.

"Quite the reverse. Should we encounter valet parking or moreover must use a valet to tour a suburban property, that's likely a sign of a parking dilemma. Expect problems."

"I'll need to write that down," stated a concerned Mike.

Jason carried on with another warning, "A less subtle hint of a potential parking predicament is when the leasing agent calls ahead of the tour with instructions of where to park. Not always, but this may be because the leasing agent knows finding an open parking space will be difficult due to over allocated parking or too many compact parking spaces. Perhaps a space has been dedicated for 'leasing'?"

> abstain from signing a lease with no reference to parking

"I would have missed that one for sure," said an appreciative Mike.

"Lastly, and most importantly," added Jason, "abstain from signing a lease with no reference to parking. You will need recourse in the event your employees and visitors cannot park on the property." And with that last statement, the parking questions and answers came to an end.

An informed tenant advisor can save you time and future parking dilemmas by understanding your parking needs and having an awareness of the parking conditions in the market. While the parking discourse focused on parking charges, Mike made a mental note to ask Jason to review his monthly rent invoice to see how much rent he was currently paying. He was sure parking was free, but he had other questions he needed answered.

4

Full Service or NNN Lease – What's Included in the Rent?

When I think of the phrase "full service," I still conjure up childhood memories of pulling into a gas station and having an attendant approach the car to fill the gas, clean the windshield, and check the car's fluids. Long gone are the days of full-service gas stations; my kids have never experienced this slice of the American experience, but the phrase "full service" is still in predominant use in the commercial real estate industry.

When a property owner quotes rental rates based on a full-service lease, what does it mean? And what is a triple net lease (or "NNN" for short)? Have you ever heard of modified gross? Mike's landlord would convert from a full-service lease to an NNN lease. "What did this entail for the software company?" was the question Mike asked of his tenant advisor, Jason Woods. This chapter will provide a brief and simple summary of Mike and Jason's dialogue during the question and answer portion of the kick-off meeting about the two major classifications of lease structures.

Full Service Lease

After a brief bio-break, Mike and Jason re-convened in Mike's office to continue their discussion.

"Mike, let's consider the phrase *full-service lease* which is sometimes called a 'gross' lease," started Jason thankful for the water bottle in hand. "In a full-service lease, everything is generally included in the base rent."

"Everything including sales tax?" asked Mike.

"Well, depending on your state, sales tax may not be included," answered Jason.

"Ok, so what do I pay for in a full-service lease?"

> **The rent in a full-service lease is an all-inclusive number**

"The rent in a full-service lease is an all-inclusive number which includes the sum of the base rent and all the operating costs for the property."

"What would be considered an operating cost for the property?" asked Mike.

"The operating costs include the property real estate taxes and insurance. Both are included in a full-service lease," answered Jason.

"What about electricity and water?" queried Mike.

"The utility cost for both the tenant spaces and common areas are included in the full-service base rental rate," answered Jason. Taking a sip of water, he continued. "The management fees, janitorial cost, landscaping, repairs and maintenance, and other ancillary costs spent to run the property are included in the base rent of a full-service lease. These costs can be expressed with the term operating expenses (OPEX)."

"In a full-service lease, the landlord pays for everything? The tenant just pays the rent?" asked Mike liking what he heard about a full-service lease.

"Yes," acknowledged Jason. "In a full-service lease, the base rent a property owner charges takes into account the cost to run the property plus the profitable income to the landlord. The operating costs are 'baked in' to the final rental rate."

Jason expounded, "For example, let's consider Property A which uses a full-service lease and quotes a rental rate of thirty dollars per square foot. A ten thousand square foot lease will yield an annual base rental of $300,000 (ten thousand times thirty dollars per square foot) or $25,000 per month. Suppose the operating expenses for the property were twelve dollars per square foot or $120,000 annually. The base rent portion (aka profit) for the landlord would be eighteen dollars per square foot or $180,000 annually (thirty dollars less the OPEX of twelve dollars). Are you with me so far, Mike?" interjected Jason.

"I believe so; please continue."

"In a full-service lease, both the base rent portion of eighteen dollars (sometimes referred to as Net Operating Income or 'NOI') plus the OPEX of twelve dollars are totaled to arrive at the thirty dollars per square foot full-service rent."

"That's great, so I don't have to worry about any property expenses in a full-service lease?"

"Well, kind of. A quick disclaimer regarding a full-service lease," cautioned Jason, "while a full-service lease provides for an all-inclusive approach to rent, the operating expenses are conjoined to a base year."

"That's a phrase the leasing agent threw my way at lunch—I think that was before his tie hit my meatball. What's a base year?"

Before Jason could answer, someone frantically stepped into Mike's office, "Mike, there's a Bob, the Closer on the line—he said it was an emergency!"

Mike glared at Jason for what seemed like hours. The look quickly turned from a frown to a smile as Mike and Jason enjoyed a good chuckle. "Please forward the call to my voice mail. Thanks."

"Ok, but he was really pushy; it seems like a life-and-death situation."

"No worries, I assure you there's no emergency," said Mike. "That Bob is persistent even after I told him I am working with another broker—he calls every day!"

"He tries hard," remarked Jason as he tried to never speak unkind words of a competitor—even Bob, the Closer. Jason can still recall the words of his old pastor, "When you point a finger at someone, three fingers point back at you."

Base Year

"Anyway, the base year is typically the year the lease began and will be the basis for all OPEX," said Jason navigating the conversation back to the discussion before Bob called. "In future lease years, the OPEX will be compared to the operating expenses for the base year." He continued, "In our thirty dollars per square foot full-service example, the twelve dollars per square foot OPEX is conjoined to a base year—the year the lease commenced. This means that in the second lease year and each subsequent year of the lease, the OPEX will be compared to the base year's twelve-dollar OPEX to determine if a shortage or surplus exist. Should a future year's OPEX be greater, then the tenant would pay its proportionate share of those increases and…"

"Sorry to interrupt. What would cause the OPEX to increase?"

"No worries, Mike. Good question," replied Jason. "Perhaps the electric company raised the kilowatts per hour charge, or the property insurance premium spiked. Or, as in your current landlord's case, perhaps the property recently sold at a higher value increasing the tax base for the property."

"Yikes!" blurted Mike.

"Yeah, we'll need to pay attention to your OPEX this upcoming year. Your current lease provides no protection against OPEX increases."

"Can you provide me an example of how this works in real life?"

"Sure. To keep it simple, if in the second year of the lease, the OPEX increased to twelve-fifty per square foot (a fifty cent per square foot increase compared to the base year of twelve dollars per square foot), then the landlord would pass the fifty cents per square foot increase to the tenant during the next calendar year."

Jason wrapped up the conversation on full-service rents. Mike had all his questions answered during the question and answer portion of the kick-off meeting, and the two called it a day. They agreed to meet later in the week to settle on the next steps for the software company.

The next morning, Mike pulled out a copy of his lease agreement eager to read it given his new understanding of usable and rentable square feet, parking ratios, and full-service lease structures. The software company had just started the final year of the lease term. He didn't make it past the second page which contained a detailed base rental schedule outlining the monthly and annual base rent for each lease year. His gaze quickly proceeded to the current year in the base rental schedule, and he noticed the monthly figure did not match the monthly billing by the landlord. *That's not what I am currently paying,* thought Mike. The landlord's rent invoice was more detailed, more complicated, and *more rent* than the monthly figure in the lease. *Am I being overbilled?*

Mike pulled the previous month's rent statement and noticed an additional $1,570 in rent due labeled Additional Rent. *What is this Additional Rent?* questioned Mike. *I thought my lease was a full-service lease?* Unfortunately, his thoughts of the landlord overbilling his

33

company clouded his recollection of the base year conversation with Jason

Mike immediately telephoned Tony Di Proprietario, the leasing agent, to discuss the rent discrepancy. Tony picked up the phone on the first ring.

"Tony, it's Mike Johnson of the software company."

"Mr. Johnson, it so nice to hear from you. I truly enjoyed our lunch together," answered Tony.

"Yes, thank you again for lunch. The reason..." began Mike.

"Did you ever engage a tenant advisor?" asked a probing Tony.

"I did, yes," responded Mike. "Jason Woods will represent the software company."

"Good choice. We've signed a few deals with Jason in the past. He's a good broker," said Tony relieved Mike didn't hire Bob, the Closer.

"Thanks," responded Mike and then he drew the conversation back to his reason for calling. "So, listen, Tony, I was reviewing my lease, which you said was a full-service lease, right?"

"That's correct."

"All right then, if my lease is full service, then it appears we've been overpaying by $1,570 per month in additional rent," said Mike. "The base rental schedule in the lease doesn't mention any additional rent, and I thought we had an all-inclusive lease."

"Great question, Mr. Johnson," responded Tony. "Want to meet tomorrow for lunch to discuss your lease?"

"No, I don't have time tomorrow, but I need to find out what's going on with the additional rent overpayments," explained Mike. "It looks like we've been paying additional rent since the second lease year and no one at the software company questioned the monthly statements."

"Well, uh, let me do this," replied Tony. "I'll have Lily, our property manager, reach out to you to explain the monthly billings. That's her department. I don't meddle with the billings."

Later that afternoon, Lily paid a visit to Mike's office. At least the property manager had a firm grasp of the monthly rent invoice (and a copy of the lease file), and they met in the conference room.

"Mr. Johnson, it's a pleasure to meet you finally," started Lily. "Tony, our leasing agent, informed me you had a question about the additional rent in your monthly statement."

"Yes, I do," interjected Mike. "I can't figure out why my monthly rent statement doesn't match the base rent schedule in the lease. There's an additional $1,570 monthly charge that shouldn't be there. It looks like we've been over-billed each month since the second lease year."

"I understand the rent statement can be a little ambiguous," answered Lily. She continued, "The software company's base year was set four years ago. The operating expenses are estimated for each lease year and then compared to the base year's operating expenses. If the current operating expense estimates are higher than the base year's operating expenses, tenants are notified and billed monthly for their proportionate share of the increases. That's the $1,570 on your monthly statement labeled Additional Rent."

"Ok, so I need to pay $1,570 per month because the estimated OPEX for the property today is $1,570 more per month than what the operating expenses were four years ago?" asked Mike finally connecting the dots from yesterday's conversation with Jason regarding the base year.

"BINGO!" said Lily nearly jumping off her chair, elated that a tenant comprehended her explanation on the first try—which never happens.

"Ah, *that's* what my broker meant yesterday when he said a full-service lease is conjoined to a base year." Mike spoke this thought out loud so that Lily heard the statement.

"Yes, he's right. It sounds like you have a good tenant advisor," added Lily.

"Great, thank you, Lily," answered Mike. "You mentioned the software company is to pay a proportionate share. Could you please explain what a proportionate share is?"

Proportionate Share

"Yes, of course, Mr. Johnson. The proportionate share, also known as percentage share, is the percentage of the property that a tenant occupies," replied Lily delighted to accommodate Mike's question. "The software company occupies fifteen thousand rentable square feet of the total two hundred thousand square foot property. Therefore, your proportionate share is 7.5 percent (fifteen thousand divided by two hundred thousand). The software company is responsible for 7.5 percent of any increase in the total operating expenses of the property above your base year which for this year is $1,570 per month."

"Well, this was helpful," said Mike. "Thank you for clarifying that for me. I believe I understand."

"My pleasure, Mr. Johnson. Anytime, we are here to serve," finished Lily. As she said her goodbyes, she noticed a light bulb out in the conference room. "Mr. Johnson, I'll send maintenance right up to change that bulb for you."

"Thank you, Lily, it was a pleasure meeting with you."

Mike now understood the inner workings and functions of a full-service lease and a base year. However, Tony, the leasing agent, mentioned the landlord would transition the property from a full-service lease structure to an NNN lease structure. How will operating expenses work in a triple net lease?

NNN Lease

Mike reached his tenant advisor on his cell phone later that day.

"In a triple net lease (NNN for short), the operating expense portion is fragmented from the base rent portion," explained Jason. "The tenant pays for both the base rent portion and all the property expenses separately."

"Jason, I'll need an example."

"For instance, Property B has a ten thousand square foot space with an NNN base rental rate of eighteen dollars per square foot," said Jason.

"Sounds like a good deal."

"Not exactly. Notice, the rate doesn't include the OPEX of twelve dollars per square foot," remarked Jason. "The sum is the same thirty dollars per square foot due in total rent as in our previous full-service Property A example."

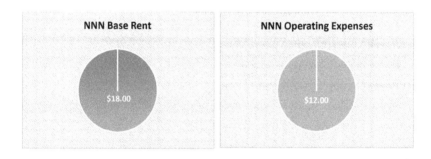

"In Property A, the tenant pays the full-service rate of thirty dollars per square foot, and the landlord pays for all the expenses to operate the property. In Property B though, the same thirty dollars per square foot total rent is reckoned, the tenant pays eighteen dollars per square foot base rent and then pays another twelve dollars per square foot for the operating expenses," explained Jason.

"At the end of the day, it sounds the same to me," rebutted Mike.

"Though this may seem like semantics, one main difference between NNN and full service is the lack of a base year," replied Jason. He continued, "Whatever the future operating expenses turn out to be, the tenant will pay that number in addition to the base rent portion. Triple net leases are commonly found in retail and industrial leases, but more and more office markets are adopting NNN lease structures."

"Why would my current landlord convert to an NNN lease?"

"Not sure other than that's how this landlord operates their leases in other markets. But not all NNN lease structures are the same," said Jason whose cell phone was now warm next to his ear. "In multi-tenant office buildings, essentially an NNN lease functions similar to a full-service lease. The real estate taxes, property insurance, and all expenses to operate the property (often referred to as common area maintenance or CAM) are pulled together and paid for by the landlord and then billed to the individual tenants based on their proportionate share. In single occupant properties, such as a drug store, the tenant is billed directly for the real estate taxes, property insurance, and common area maintenance. The landlord just collects the base rent portion."

Mike asked Jason, "Which is more beneficial to my company, a full-service lease or an NNN lease?"

"A full-service lease is a two-sided coin with a benefit on one side and hurt on the other. On the benefit side of the coin, a full-service lease gives a business owner a simplified all in one number to work with and budget for, while providing the hedge of a fixed base year. And since the profits are directly correlated to the amount of the OPEX, landlords have an incentive to operate the properties effectively and efficiently. In contrast, in an NNN lease, the base rent portion (or profit) is fixed for landlords regardless of the OPEX."

"Ok, what's the other side of the coin?"

"On the hurt side, a full-service lease allows a landlord to double dip on the annual increases in both the base rent and the OPEX portion," responded Jason.

"What do you mean by double dip?"

"With a 3 percent annual increase, the 3 percent applies to the full-service rate of thirty dollars per square foot. The landlord enjoys a 3 percent increase on both the base rent portion and the OPEX portion resulting in a ninety-cent per square foot increase in year two. In an NNN lease, the annual increase of 3 percent would only apply to the base rent portion of eighteen dollars per square foot resulting in a fifty-four cent per square foot increase in year two," answered Jason.

Mike took notes.

"Another negative factor of a full-service lease is the potential effect of an abnormally low base year. A low base year can devastate a business owner in future lease years."

"How can a property have a low base year?" quizzed Mike.

"Many factors can impact a property's operating expenses resulting in a low base year. Large vacancies or a low property tax assessment can artificially set a base year far below market operating expense."

"Why is a low base year considered on the negative side of the coin?" followed up Mike standing up from his desk to stretch his legs as the conversation continued.

"Because the lower the base year, the more likely the landlord will pass future and substantive OPEX increases to tenants," replied Jason. "For example, a mostly vacant property that increases occupancy during the lease term or the sale of a property resulting in a higher taxable value can both result in drastic increases in the building's operating expenses. And remember, those increases will be proportionately passed on to the tenants of the property," responded Jason.

"Hmm," sounded Mike over the cell phone.

"Suppose," explained Jason, "the average OPEX in the market for a stabilized property was twelve dollars per square foot. A newly constructed property still paying real estate taxes based on land values will lead to a low base year of eight dollars per square foot for the OPEX. Got it?"

"Yes, got it."

"Therefore, in future years of the lease, as the occupancy stabilizes and the real estate taxes are reassessed, the OPEX will catch up to the market OPEX of twelve dollars per square foot," continued Jason.

"You mean the tenants will have to pay an additional four dollars per square foot for the difference between the twelve-dollar OPEX and the eight dollars per square foot base year?" questioned an enlightened Mike.

"That's correct, Mike."

"Unreal! That would devastate our business and profit margins," exclaimed Mike. "An increase like that could get me fired! Jason, that's overwhelming."

"Exactly," retorted Jason. "That's why I'm here. We won't sign any lease without scrutinizing the operating expense provisions."

Jason and Mike brought the conversation to a close. By now Mike Johnson had his fill of full service and NNN leases, and Jason Woods' cell phone battery was nearly dead. The conversation convinced Mike that he wanted to keep the status quo and remain in a full-service lease structure.

Additional variations can exist in full-service leases and NNN leases. For instance, some full-service leases are "net of utilities and janitorial." This means all the expenses to operate the property are included in the rent except utilities which are separately metered and paid individually per tenant, and each tenant will contract to clean their suite. A net of utilities and janitorial lease is sometimes called "modified gross lease" with modified standing for the expenses not paid for by the landlord.

Operating expenses are one of many provisions buried deep within a lease that can have an immense impact on the affordability of a lease. For Mike's current landlord, the switch from a full-service lease to an NNN lease worked to the landlord's disadvantage. The other properties the software company toured within the marketplace all quoted rents on a full-service lease. Mike's existing landlord, having recently purchased the property, gave no consideration to market conditions. Business owners in the market simply did not understand the NNN lease structure and were highly skeptical.

Much more can be said about operating expenses, including caps on controllable expenses, operating expense exclusions, and how to avoid an abnormally low base year. A knowledgeable and experienced real estate advisor can provide substantive insight to protect and hedge against increasing operating expenses. Mike Johnson and Jason Woods purposed to tour properties that only featured full-service leases.

5

When Should I Start Looking for Space?

The time to look for space will vary depending on company size and/ or layout of the space. The larger the tenant, the longer the time to implement a transition to a new space. A twenty thousand square foot company will need significantly more time and preparation than a two thousand square foot company.

The same can be said of a company, regardless of size, with a layout scheme that does not match the norm for the submarket. For instance, a two thousand square foot technology company seeking an open plan with exposed ceilings and concrete floors in a submarket of predominantly service providers such as accountants and law firms, will also need more time and preparation than a typical two thousand square foot company.

"When should we look for space?" Mike asked his tenant advisor, Jason Woods.

"In optimal conditions, a company should not look for space until much consideration and planning has taken place before ever 'hitting the road' to tour potential office locations," answered Jason. He continued, "The planning and plotting before endeavoring to tour space can be thought of as the pre-tour phase—it's referenced in the kick-off checklist."

"I've never heard of a pre-tour phase," began Mike, "what does this entail?"

Pre-tour Phase

"The pre-tour phase will include a thorough review of the current size and layout of the office and compare it to your future office space needs to surmise the right size for your office. It will also take into account the best submarket and properties to tour," answered Jason. "Think of the pre-tour phase as a map providing direction for the rest of the journey toward the lease execution date."

Road map leading to signing of lease

Jason handed Mike a sheet labeled "The Pre-tour Phase," which he later emailed to him. The sheet contained an itemized list with three headings: size requirement, location, and budget.

"Wow! This list is rather detailed," commented Mike.

"Potential tenants must consider and address all the questions raised in the pre-tour phase list to make potential tours more efficient and successful," responded Jason. "Understanding the ideal size, location, and base rental budget will provide an effective course of action in selecting a future office."

Jason elaborated, "As we'll see, the use of a professional space planner or architect is beneficial to establish the ideal layout and growth potential of your firm. Any cost associated with this step is minuscule compared to the savings a creative architect can achieve by reviewing and designing your ideal and most efficient space. Both the architect and I can speak to current industry size standards and trends."

"Perfect," echoed Mike. "Let's start the process."

Mike Johnson and Jason Woods spent the next week in diligent deliberations, reviewing the pre-tour phase sheet and answering the questions raised. Mike involved his Human Research Department and key software engineers to understand what was important to the firm. Though Mike was eager to tour spaces, skipping this process could lead to much wasted time, frustration, and overpayment of rent in future days. By carefully conducting the pre-tour phase, Jason was adequately prepared to survey the market for properties which most represented the ideal conditions for the software company.

Mike asked another question, "How long will it take to move once I sign a lease?"

"Customarily, at least six to eight months is recommended for the average sized company to transition to a new space, which would be your case," replied Jason. "A company in need of larger space for their business will need to stretch this period out up to twelve–eighteen months."

"Why so long?"

Jason answered, "The time accounts for the property tours, negotiations of proposals, space planning, lease negotiations and signing, the tenant improvements, and implementing the move to the new office."

"Jason, that still seems like a long time. Are you sure we need eight months to relocate?"

"A simple way to figure out how long it will take to move into a new office," expounded Jason, "is to work backward from your lease expiration or desired move-in date. If…"

"How so? I bet you were going to answer before I interrupted. Sorry."

"No worries. If January 1 is the targeted move-in date, we can assume a build-out of the office (the necessary modifications to make a space occupiable) will typically take twelve weeks or three months. Permits required for the build-out can take up to six–eight weeks or longer depending on the municipality. The architect and engineers will need at least four weeks to complete the construction drawings once the space plan is approved and the lease is signed. A standard lease may take up to thirty days to negotiate and execute. Add up all the times, and we end up with approximately seven months for an average-sized business to move into their new space once a property is selected," explained Jason to an overwhelmed Mike.

"My lease expires at the end of the year, when should we have a signed lease to move out on time?"

"Funny you should ask, Mike," stated Jason, "I just happened to prepare a timeline schedule for your review." Jason pulled a file out of his backpack and unfolded a legal-sized sheet on Mike's desk entitled, "The software company timeline." The timeline incorporated, on a line item basis, the steps necessary to move into new space, and correlated each step with a date on the calendar. Key elements and dates such as signing the lease, permit approval, and construction completion were highlighted in red.

"According to the timeline, we must have a letter of intent or proposal agreed upon and signed no later than June 1, with a lease execution date of no later than July 1 to make a January 1 move-in date," answered Jason.

"I never realized all that went into relocating an office. Jason, I'm glad we're working together because I would have assumed ninety days at best to move," confessed Mike as he continued to review the timeline. He added, "Is there anything that can slow down the process?"

"Absolutely. A labor strike, a disaster, shortage of materials, or a delay in the permit process can certainly delay the time frame," stated Jason. He continued, "On the other hand, an astute contractor or a witty landlord willing to start the construction drawings early or a build-out which does not require a permit, can also shorten the time frame considerably. Hence, we should allocate around eight months to move into a new space."

"I understand now why you've scheduled properties tours for next week. We still have eight months before our lease expiration," interjected Mike.

"Yes, and keep in mind; this time frame to relocate is well known by landlords and their leasing agents."

> **Leverage is key to negotiating with your current Landlord**

Mike wanted to know, "Is that negative?"

"Leverage is key to negotiating with your current landlord or a potential new landlord. If these time frames are not adhered to and lessened in duration, the leverage will sway toward the landlord's favor."

"What's the worst that can happen to a tenant if they wait too long?" asked Mike.

"Regrettably, not every business owner or decision maker realizes the importance of allowing for a proper time cushion to permit a relocation. The examples are numerous."

Jason then mentioned the following example of a business owner who waited too long to search for space.

"A law firm occupying nearly five thousand rentable square feet in a tightening submarket with limited vacancies assumed they could wait until ninety days before their expiration to discuss a possible renewal with the landlord. After all, the law firm had been a good paying tenant for many years.

They approached the landlord to review the possibility of extending the lease for another five years. At the meeting, the law firm experienced sticker shock at the new quoted rental rates, nearly 30 percent higher than what they had signed up for five years prior. The tenant presented a counteroffer to the landlord; five dollars per rentable square foot lower than what the landlord was seeking. No surprise, the landlord held firm to the quoted rate.

The law firm scrambled to tour alternative space options and was surprised to find limited opportunities. The few spaces they toured were quoting the same or higher rental rates, but there was one property currently under renovations offering a discounted rent to attract tenants. The property featured more amenities and better views than their current office. Only one problem: the space would require substantial improvements. The alternative property owner could not deliver the space substantially complete in less than six months –"

"What does substantially complete mean?" asked Mike.

"Substantially complete means the space is a fully constructed (except minor items known as punch list items) and ready for occupancy with the proper governmental approvals in hand," answered Jason and he returned to the story. "Though the space was ideal and provided significant rent savings, the law firm had to walk away from this great opportunity. The law firm had no choice but to sign the five-year renewal with their current landlord at the business terms proposed by the landlord."

Jason ended the story by adding, "An experienced landlord or leasing agent will know if adequate time remains for a tenant to relocate their office. If too little time remains on the lease, a business owner should expect fewer incentives. Worse, provisions like holdover tenancy (occupancy following the expiration of the term) and double rent may also become a factor."

If you own a business or are a decision maker, let me plead with you: get a tenant advisor on your side. The fine-tuned efforts of a tenant advisor to guide the pre-tour phase and then to activate and execute the plan will result in selecting the most optimum office property for your business. Signing a lease with the proper time allotment to allow for the future space to be improved and a move to be coordinated will depend greatly on the effective work of your tenant advisor.

Fortunately, Mike engaged Jason Woods who guided the software company through the pre-tour phase enabling Mike to determine the proper size for the firm, location, and budget for the office. During the pre-tour phase, Mike sought the help of an architect, at Jason's recommendation. Based on industry standards and trends, Mike and the architect concluded the software company's ideal space requirement should be approximately eight thousand to eighty-five hundred usable square feet or ten thousand rentable square feet, 50 percent less than their current full floor office.

Mike envisioned a more collaborative and mobile workforce than what his current office permitted. Though he planned on adding key talent to the firm, through shared work areas, virtual and office hoteling, and communal environments, the actual office size could substantially decrease from the current full floor the software company occupied. *Unreal, what a potential savings in rent,* thought Mike. *I bet the board members would be impressed with that!* He was already reaping the benefits of hiring a tenant advisor, and to think Jason Woods' fee would be paid for by the landlord where the software company signs a lease.

With eight months remaining on the current lease, as long as the strict timeline Jason Woods plotted out was adhered to, Mike Johnson would peacefully transition to a new space.

Mike was no longer overwhelmed. He shed the title of *OBO*—Overwhelmed Business Owner, and was on his way toward triumph. He then remembered his grandmother's wise words from the Bible, "Where no counsel is, the people fall; but in the multitude of counsellors there is safety" (Proverbs 11:14, KJV).

6

Does TI Stand for Too Much Information?

Tony Di Proprietario had informed Mike Johnson at lunch "if he needed TI the landlord would be happy to accommodate." Mike was overwhelmed with all the commercial real estate talk abruptly thrown his way; TI might as well have meant too much information. But as my kids remind me, too much information is known as the acronym "TMI" and not "TI." I have ventured not to offer TMI with this book, but rather "RI," relevant information. Having already answered the question of the chapter, let's take a deeper dive into this two-letter acronym "TI."

TI stands for tenant improvements.

TI stands for tenant improvements. Property owners and brokers will often mention TI during the property tours, typically asking "What TI will you need?" Proposals will feature sections referencing TI or perhaps TIA. Bob, the Closer promised Mike he could get him a "hefty TI package."

"So, what does TI stand for and how does it impact my business?" was the next question Mike raised to Jason Woods, his tenant advisor, over an espresso at a trendy coffee shop near the office.

"The search for a possible business home does not end at signing a lease. Usually, the space leased will need to be modified to meet your business needs before occupying the space," warmly stated Jason. He enjoyed providing expert analysis to his clients (and a good espresso). "Such modifications to the space can vary from as little as paint and carpet to as complex as a full build-out involving permits, plans, and months of construction. This build-out, whether large or small, necessary to modify the leased space for your occupancy is known as tenant improvements or TI for short."

"That simplifies it, thanks," replied Mike finishing his espresso.

Jason continued, "Well, two main questions arise when considering TI. How much will the TI cost and who pays for the modifications to the space, the landlord or the tenant?"

"Yes, my two questions exactly, Jason. You took the words out of my mouth," quickly corresponded Mike.

Jason knew he hit a pressure point with the two questions, "Tenant improvements are a key feature to any negotiations and can have a tremendous impact on the lease value. The answers to the questions of how much will the TI cost and who pays for the TI are consequential to a business owner's decision to lease or not lease a space."

"Got it. Where do we start?"

TI Cost

Jason continued, "Let's deal initially with the question how much will the TI cost to make a space habitable for business use. First, not every space is the same and each space we will tour may require entirely different tenant improvements. Some spaces offer a beneficial layout and existing improvements left over from a previous tenant which can be reclaimed for future tenants."

"Such as?"

"Ceiling grids and tiles, light fixtures, walls, cabinetry, marble floors, kitchens, doors and frames, electric, and plumbing can all be used by future tenants," responded Jason as he too was out of espresso. "On the other hand, some spaces will require demolition of all the existing improvements to reconstruct the new space."

Jason paused the conversation to go to the counter and order two more espressos.

"Still other spaces may require a full build-out, as in newly constructed buildings, which are in raw condition, meaning no improvements exist such as walls and ceilings as the space has never been built out or has recently been demolished," said Jason returning to the table with the second round of espressos. "All that to say the tenant improvement cost can vary dramatically from property to property."

"Jason, you know my next question: who pays for the TI?" asked Mike as he opened a brown sugar pack and added it to his espresso.

"Good thing we refilled our coffees as here's where the rubber meets the road," answered Jason. "Mike, I apologize in advance, as I'll need a few minutes to describe how this works, but it's important."

Mike nodded with approval as he sipped his coffee (though his nodding could have easily been his approval of the savory taste of his refilled espresso).

Jason began, "Generally, the landlord will pay for reasonable TI cost. However, tenant improvements will impact other business points of a deal such as base rent, free rent, and length of the term. Regarding term, the more dollars a landlord spends to build-out or modify the space, the longer the lease because the landlord amortizes or spreads out the TI cost over the lease years. Greater TI, longer term. Lower TI, shorter term."

Another nod from Mike, and another sip.

"Mike, if your objective, due to growth or uncertainty, is to sign a maximum lease term of three years, then finding a space that requires little TI will be the objective. If you are agreeable to a term of five to ten years, then, depending on market conditions, the landlords may pay for all the TI cost as they will have more years to recoup their build-out expenses."

"How much will a landlord be willing to pay for the TI?"

"The amount a landlord will pay for TI or provide in a TIA will vary from market to market and not only depends on the length of the term but also usually correlates to the amount of rent being charged. The higher the rent, the larger the TIA. The lower the rent, the lower the TIA."

> **TIA will vary from market to market**

"Okay, slow down, what's a TIA? I recall Tony, the leasing agent, mentioning TIA at lunch as well."

"Thanks for asking. TIA stands for tenant improvement allowance. The tenant improvement allowance is the total dollars a landlord will contribute toward the tenant improvements," replied Jason. "Typically, TIA will be larger in a newly constructed property as more dollars are needed to finish a raw space (a space that is not improved) than a second-generation space (a space that has been improved in the past).

Another factor playing a role in the amount of TIA a landlord will contribute is whether the current economy presents *landlord* favorable conditions or *tenant*-favorable conditions," mentioned Jason.

"Could you describe these conditions, please?"

"Sure. In a landlord favorable market, high occupancy or peak times will trend toward landlords increasing rental rates and reducing incentives which include lower TIA. Conversely, in a tenant-favorable market, high vacancy will trend toward stagnant or falling rents and an increase in incentives by landlords to attract tenants including larger TIA," explained Jason. He added the example that during the late 2000's in Miami, although similar situations happened in many places, with the delivery of two million square feet of office space combined with a national recession, Brickell Avenue and downtown Miami experienced dramatic tenant-favorable conditions. Landlords were offering markedly higher TIA than under normal conditions. Some properties provided more than double the standard tenant improvements during stabilized conditions to attract tenants.

"Wow! What kind of market condition exist today in our area?" questioned an excited Mike.

"We're far removed from the Great Recession and closer to equilibrium. We'll need to do our homework and diligence to achieve the most TIA," answered Jason as the two finished their conversation and second round of espressos.

With the pre-tour phase completed, Jason unearthed six potential properties for the software company to tour that could accommodate their requirement. Given that eight months remained until the lease expiration, all build-out options were on the table for Mike.

"Mike, I've set the tours for next Friday morning."

"Excellent," responded Mike. "Where do we meet?"

"I'll swing by your office fifteen minutes before the start of the tours," answered Jason. "See you on Friday, God willing."

At last, the day of the tour arrived, and Jason picked up Mike early on Friday morning. Jason presented the property tour book to Mike which included a map report, property brochures, and floor plans for all six properties on the tour. The tour commenced at 9 a.m. and continued every half hour throughout the morning hours. After the last property tour, they headed back to Mike's office for a working lunch to discuss the tours. In the meeting, Mike, with Jason's insight and guidance, narrowed down the short list to three possible properties for further consideration:

- Space Option A was recently occupied by a high-end competitor and featured a very similar layout to the software company's current office. Other than finishes, such as paint, carpet, and perhaps upgraded tile in the reception area, the space worked great.

- Space Option B has been on the market for several months. The last occupant was in the space for many years, and the dated space featured large inefficient offices and toured like a maze. Jason even lost Mike during the tour and had to call his cell phone to find him. The property recently upgraded all the building standards, so everything in the space including the ceiling grid and tiles, light fixtures, and doors will need to be replaced. The space will require a full demolition.
- Space Option C is a new property that featured a full floor for lease. The space was in raw condition. With no improvements to work with, the space will require a full build-out.

Determining the TI Cost

Back to the question at hand, how much will the TI cost for each of the properties? With a cursory glance at these three options, Mike discerned Space Option A would require less capital than Space Option B and C. Yet it was still imperative for comparison purposes, to calculate what the tenant improvements will cost to verify if the tenant improvement allowance provided by the landlords would cover the tenant improvements needed for each space.

Jason recommended the use of the same architect, who previously worked with the software company on the pre-tour phase, to do the "test-fit" space plan for all three properties—though the landlords preferred to use their architects. Using one architect, as opposed to three landlord architects, provided a better comparison of each space utilizing the same program and philosophy, and prevented Mike Johnson from having to meet with three different professionals for each step of the process.

For Space Option A, the test-fit space plan just entailed confirming the layout worked and deciding what still needs to be modified such as finishes. However, for Space Options B and C, the process was more involved as the architect reinvented the space to match Mike's requirement.

Once the test fits were complete based on the software company's space program, Mike reviewed and approved the plans for all three properties. Jason then released all three space plans to the three properties who, during the proposal negotiation phase, separately priced out the tenant improvements with their respective general contractors. Ultimately, they would obtain three bids, but in this early stage, one contractor price sufficed. Depending on the size and sophistication, a tenant may elect to control the bid process, but the norm is for the landlord to obtain pricing. In Mike's case, he was glad not to dedicate his after-hours to coordinating the contractor bid process.

One week later, Jason received the construction bids from the properties and forwarded them to Mike.

- Space Option A will cost $50,000 in TI necessary to modify the space for the software company's use. The TI entailed new carpet and paint and upgraded flooring in the reception area. Therefore, a tenant improvement allowance (TIA) of five dollars per square foot will be needed to pay for the tenant improvements ($50,000/10,000 SF).
- Space Option B will cost $400,000 in TI necessary to modify the space for the software company's use. The entire space will be demolished, and except for a few savings such as sprinkler heads and HVAC systems, the office would be primarily a new space. Therefore, a TIA of forty dollars per square foot would be needed to pay for the tenant improvements.
- Space Option C will cost $500,000 in TI necessary to modify the space for the software company's use. The space is considered "first generation space." In other words, everything in the space will be constructed new and tailored for the purpose and

use of the software company. Hence, a TIA of fifty dollars per square foot will be needed to pay for the tenant improvements.

Jason prepared a TI cost analysis which included the total estimated cost of the TI as compared to the TIA each landlord offered. After the TI cost review, Mike Johnson leaned toward Space Option C, though he preferred to lease Space Option B. But the landlord at Space Option B would not offer more than a thirty dollar per square foot TIA or $300,000 toward the tenant improvements leaving the software company to pay for the balance of the tenant improvements totaling $100,000 (total TI cost needed of forty dollars per square foot with the landlord only offering a thirty dollar per square foot TIA left ten dollars per square foot for the tenant to pay). Space Option A proved to be the cost leader considering the minimal TI needed, but in the end, Mike desired to provide his stamp on the new office.

Space Option C provided the full fifty dollars per square foot TIA, the $500,000 needed to improve the space for the software company's use. Determining how much the TI will cost and who will pay for the TI are vital questions to answer before signing any lease, and may ultimately decide where a company locates the office.

Turnkey Build-out

Mike raised another concern to Jason, "But what if the tenant improvement cost exceeds fifty dollars per square foot at Space Option C, how can I assure the software company doesn't get nickeled and dimed to pay for overages?"

"Great point," replied Jason, "We can always request a turnkey build-out."

"I'm sorry. Did you say *turkey* build-out or *turnkey*?" asked Mike a little confused with Jason's response.

Turkey Construction

"*Turnkey*," answered Jason with a smile. "While a tenant improvement allowance provides the total dollars a landlord is willing to spend on tenant improvements, a turnkey build-out stipulates the landlord will do and pay for all the tenant improvements. The tenant improvements will be by mutually agreed upon plans and specifications which will be attached to the lease document as an exhibit. The landlord may further set forth certain specifications which are to be included such as building standard finishes."

"But it's important that I choose the color schemes of the finishes as I'm trying to enhance our brand image in the space," contested Mike worried the landlord would have a say in the carpet and paint colors of his space.

Jason quickly added, "Though the building has a defined standard for materials to be used in each space, the tenant chooses the colors of these materials. You can still have your branded color schemes throughout the space."

"Okay, I feel better now," responded Mike. "My favorite question Jason; how does this work in the real world?"

"Of course. Once you and the landlord agree to the plans and specifications, they'll be attached to the lease. That way, both the landlord and tenant know exactly what to expect in the tenant improvements. The tenant will pay any further changes to the plan which result in an increased cost," responded Jason.

Jason elaborated that a turnkey build-out allows business owners who have a firm understanding of their space program and who've thoroughly reviewed the space plan and scope of work, the peace of mind of knowing their space will be built out at no cost to them. Sizeable Fortune 500 companies, with project managers on staff and national corporate standards for tenant improvements, will typically prefer to receive a tenant improvement allowance. These large firms have project managers dedicated to building out spaces and prefer to keep the tenant improvement process uniform. But given the liability and responsibility of all the cost associated with the construction of the space sides with the landlord, a turnkey build-out is often a favorable way to handle the tenant improvements for most business owners.

You probably already figured out Mike did not renew the lease at his current location, despite the lovely lunch with the leasing agent, Tony Di Proprietario. For starters, Mike was very uncomfortable with his landlord switching from a full-service lease to an NNN lease. Second, after negotiating with the three alternative properties, he realized his current landlord was increasing the rental rate to renew far above the market. *Not sure why the leasing agent had to whisper about getting a great deal— ruining my meatball,* pondered Mike. Third, the property renovations had commenced, and Lily, the property manager, kindly informed all the tenants that the renovations would last at least two years. The dust, noise, and interruptions from the construction were too much for Mike to take. Therefore, he insisted a fresh start would be necessary. Besides, he inherited a space from his predecessor and alternate properties permitted Mike to place his imprint and vision on the software company's space.

"I like that option, that turnkey thing. Let's go down that road," affirmed Mike.

"Yes sir, I will be sure to include it in the RFP."

"Great," answered Mike. "What's an RFP?"

7

LOI Versus RFP – I'm RTG so Can You Explain?

To the best of my knowledge, using commercially reasonable efforts, brokers do not use Morse code when conducting real estate transactions. We also do not speak in pig-Latin or secret codes. Though some of us "se habla Español." So why so many phrases like "LOI" and "RFP" to name a few (we just considered TI and TIA in the previous chapter).

Many industries use time-saving acronyms in the place of often repeated phrases and names. For instance, the CEO meets with the CFO before COB to review the company's YTD KPI to boost the company's EOY P & L statements as the company considers an IPO in Q1 of the new year. Imagine how many more words would be needed to complete that statement without the acronyms substituting for the phrases and titles.

The commercial real estate industry is no different. Proposals and leases will often read SF for square feet or p.s.f. in the place of per square foot. One might find RSF for rentable square feet or CAM as a substitute for common area maintenance.

Let's return to the discourse between Jason Woods and Mike Johnson at the software company's office. "What's an RFP?" asked Mike from behind his desk.

"RFP is shorthand for *request for a proposal*. I prefer to use an RFP to commence the negotiation phase rather than asking for an LOI," responded Jason.

"And an LOI is?" asked Mike.

"LOI is simply another way of saying a proposal which summarizes the business points under consideration. LOI is shorthand for letter of intent which is the proposal negotiated between the landlord and tenant or buyer and seller," answered Jason. "While there may be many renditions of the LOI such as counter proposals, landlord proposals, and tenant counter proposals; in the end, they are all offers by one party to the other to lease the space in question."

"Do we have to negotiate with one property at a time or can we negotiate multiple proposals at once?" Mike inquired of his tenant advisor.

"I get that question often," responded Jason. "For the most part, as in 99 percent of the time, proposals are non-binding offers. Either party at any time can leave the negotiations and terminate their offers. Most proposals will include this disclaimer toward the end of the offer, and such a disclaimer should always be heeded."

"How's that a good thing if either party can walk? It seems you'll never know if you have a deal if it's not binding?"

"Mike, I understand your concern. But it's actually the opposite case," replied Jason enjoying the conversation. "The non-binding aspect of proposals is a well thought out provision wrought with good intentions. This one factor leads to good faith negotiations between both parties and levels the playing field between landlord and tenant."

Mike understood the idea of a non-binding proposal, but this raised a concern regarding locking up a space. "So, when do you know for sure that a space is yours?"

"Not until a lease is fully executed by both parties and delivered to both parties is a lease document binding and the space secure," answered Jason. "Despite this clear provision in proposals, on occasion, tenants and landlords have proceeded with plans and spent dollars based on non-binding proposals. That is not advisable."

It was now 2:30 p.m. and as if right on cue, a highly skilled (and well compensated) software engineer, with small plastic cups in one hand and a tiny metal pitcher in the other, opened Mike's door, and interrupted the meeting with a one-word question, "Cafecito?"

To those of you not familiar with this Miami ritual, "Cafecito" is a shot of Cuban coffee served in nearly every Miami office around 2:30 p.m. Somehow, every business has at least one employee who knows the intricacies of making Cuban coffee; packing in the Cuban style coffee (espresso) into the *cafetera* or stove top espresso maker, combining the right amount of sugar with the first few drops of the brewed coffee creating a wonderful foam, then stirring it all together at the completion of the brew. The entire office can smell the rich aromas as the artist masters his coffee craft.

The sweet expression of life and vitality makes its way around the office until everyone has enjoyed a small shot of Cafecito energized to finish the work day. *No one* turns down the offer.

In fact, the question is more of a statement, *"Cafecito."*

As Mike and Jason paused their conversation to savor the coffee, Mike recollected the time an out of town visitor responded, "No thanks," to the offer "Cafecito." Screech! Utter silence. The background white noise or music (doesn't matter), shut off! Everyone in the office stopped what they were doing and in unison gasped with hands covering their mouth and eyes fixated on the visitor. Mike graciously kept his composure and gave the visitor a second chance, an opportunity to recover, "Are you sure you don't want the *Cafecito*?" he asked with a cynical eye and dark tone in his voice. Each syllable in the word Cafecito seemed to carry a message of warning.

With all eyes still directed toward the visitor, he wised up and answered, "Ok, yeah, on second thought I'll take it. Thanks." After a collective sigh of relief, all was good, and the office returned to normal. Just another day in South Florida.

So, if you are visiting an office in Miami around 2:30 p.m., *take* the Cafecito! "But I don't drink coffee." No matter: Just say, "Okay," and take the tiny cup in your hand and continue your conversation. Then after some time, slowly and casually, no sudden movements, place the little cup down and carry on.

Finishing his coffee shot, Mike continued the discourse, "I want to comprehend this. First, we'll need to go through the entire negotiation process with the RFP and LOI stuff and sign that; even though it's not binding." Jason nodded his head while taking his last sip of coffee. "Then we'll need to negotiate a lease document, and once the lease the lease is signed, we have a deal?" asked Mike with a bit of contentment for following the conversation.

"Correct, but recall the lease must be signed by both parties and delivered to both parties."

"Got it. Now that we've identified three properties to pursue, the next step is to ask the landlord to prepare the RFP proposals?" asked Mike rubbing his hands together in anticipation of starting the next step.

The RFP

"Well, the RFP is a different sort of proposal. In fact, it is not a proposal at all," spoke Jason, not intentionally trying to slow his client's enthusiasm down. Jason continued, "The tenant's broker produces the RFP on behalf of the tenant. The RFP is initially forwarded to the landlord dictating the specific business points and conditions to be addressed by the landlord in their proposal response. An RFP is a solicitation to the landlord, the first shot across the bow, opening the negotiation process."

"Why start the negotiations with the RFP as opposed to receiving a standard proposal from a landlord?" asked Mike wanting to know the benefit of this additional step instead of advancing directly into the landlord proposals.

"I recently completed a transaction for a client who was referred to me, but only after they commenced the process on their own," revealed Jason. He told the following story:

The data company toured ten properties and shortlisted three of those properties to consider further. The CEO requested proposals or LOIs from the three separate leasing agents representing the three potential spaces. One proposal came the next business day from an eager landlord. The second proposal arrived one week later, and the third proposal took nearly two weeks to arrive via email. As the data company awaited the second and third proposals, the eager landlord telephoned daily for an update to the proposal submitted.

Once in possession of all three offers, the CEO reviewed the different offers. Not much time had elapsed when he had difficulty lining up all three offers for comparison. Each offer came in a different format, included different references, terminology, and points, and varied greatly. One quoted an NNN base rent, while two others were full service. One offered the space in "as is" condition, another offered paint and carpet, with the eager landlord offering a tenant improvement allowance of twenty dollars per rentable square foot. One proposal offered an option to renew, and two were silent regarding any options.

Regarding a security deposit, one proposal requested to review financial statements, another requested a personal guarantee, and the third asked for four months' deposit. All three offers varied in the length of the lease from five to seven to ten years. They also varied in the rent commencement date by several months.

None of the offers addressed the CEO's concerns for future growth, building access, signage, security, and parking. "How am I ever going to array these offers to compare them and make recommendations to my board," pondered the CEO.

All the while, three aggressive leasing agents were continuously calling and emailing, seeking updates and opportunities to meet. "When should we expect a counteroffer? Can I take you to lunch? Would you like to meet with the building owner, or receive free tickets to a game?" continued the leasing agents.

What a disaster, thought the CEO of the data company. "Is there a better way to handle the proposal negotiations?"

Help!

"Yes, there is a much better way, and the overwhelmed business owner confessed his dilemma to a business associate. It turned out, that business associate was my client, and he referred the data company to me," said Jason bringing the story to a point. "I quickly stepped in and prepared the RFP with the CEO's input."

"Nice," expressed Mike.

Jason resumed, "Why start the negotiations with the RFP? Multiple reasons exist for a business owner to first submit the RFP to a landlord rather than just ask for a proposal, as seen in the data company's example. For instance:

- RFPs allow for uniform comparisons; apples to apples comparisons on every point
- RFPs allow a tenant to dictate the specific points of interest which a landlord may miss or leave out in a standard proposal
- RFPs delineate the time expectation for responses to the proposal
- RFPs give a tenant leverage as it sets the proper tone for the negotiations reminding the landlord there are other properties under consideration

Jason continued, "Once the landlord receives the RFP, the landlord is to respond with their proposed terms and conditions using the RFP format which includes time parameters. The response process by the landlord will require an extra step and more careful thought and consideration than a standard proposal."

"How did the RFP help the data company's CEO?" probed Mike interested in the outcome.

"First, I met with the data company's CEO to accumulate the main business points we'd want all three landlords to address in the RFP," replied Jason. He proceeded, "For example, the CEO's concern for future growth, building access, signage, security, and parking were included in the RFP. What mattered most to the CEO would be front and center in the RFP. Second, all three responses by the landlords were delivered to us in a timely, uniform, and orderly format allowing for side by side, apples to apples comparison. No more trying to find misplaced pieces of a puzzle that may or may not match up."

"Third," continued Jason uninterrupted by the inquisitive Mike who by now was taking notes, "the RFP directed the landlords how to respond to each separate point such as base rent. For comparison purposes, the RFP requested the landlords quote the base rent on a grossed-up or full-service basis rather than NNN simplifying the deal cost comparisons. The RFP also ordered the tenant improvements, and informed the landlords the data company would not sign a personal guarantee."

> **the RFP directed the landlords how to respond to each separate point**

"Fourth, by using the RFP, I eliminated the number of follow-up calls and emails to the CEO because as tenant advisor, I became the single point of contact. I provided a hedge around the CEO of the data company, allowing him to run his company instead of dealing with three separate leasing agents," said Jason.

"Interesting. By no means did I take that into account. What a relief to know I won't get flooded by calls and follow ups," remarked Mike placing a large asterisk next to that point.

"A further benefit of the RFP is landlords made better offers than what the data company's CEO received directly," added Jason.

"That *is* a great benefit!" exclaimed Mike, another asterisk.

"With all the terms and conditions identified in the RFP, much anxiety and guesswork were removed from the negotiations. The RFP provided a roadmap for the landlord's leasing agents to follow permitting them to address all the hot buttons of the data company. Leverage was swayed to the data company who was now in control of the negotiation process through the RFP," said Jason.

"Leverage, I presume that is key to negotiating a favorable deal."

"Absolutely," affirmed Jason. "The RFP provided for an objective deal cost comparison which I prepared for the CEO once we received the offers from the landlord. The deal cost comparison allowed the data company to make an informed decision as to which property provided them the best value and it streamlined the recommendation process to the board."

"What does a deal cost comparison consist of?"

"Well, for starters, the deal cost comparison lines up all the key business points of each proposal side by side," answered Jason. "From usable and rentable square feet, to the monthly rents, tenant improvements, hours of operation, and security deposit, all the business items referenced in the RFP are compared. The deal cost comparison can also review the effective rates of each deal." Sensing he walked too deep into the woods at the mention of effective rates, Jason added, "The effective rate starts with the rental rate and factors in incentives such as free rent and TIA. Some prefer to add a discount rate to this figure to arrive at a net present value of each offer."

"Glad you will be the one putting this all together, and I'm sure it will make more sense once we begin the negotiation process."

"Others like to use more involved financial software to analyze the offers. Whichever comparison method is used, without the RFP, a deal cost comparison would be impossible," continued Jason. "And the deal cost comparison will time stamp each offer and counteroffer by both parties. That way, a business owner can track the progress and savings achieved during the negotiations and objectively know they're getting a good deal."

Jason ended the discussion with a closing remark. "The main difference between an LOI and an RFP is control. Who will control the

The RFP allows the tenant to control the process

negotiation process, the landlord or the tenant? The RFP allows the tenant to control the process from start to finish."

Fully convinced of the need to commence the negotiations with the RFP, Mike and Jason discussed the many business points and conditions to include in the software company RFP. A skilled tenant advisor will know the importance of utilizing an RFP and will include the business points that matter most to your business.

Understanding commercial real estate acronyms isn't as complicated as cracking a secret code or sending a Morse code signal; at least not when you have a professional representing your real estate needs. Just in case you were wondering, the following is Morse code for LOI and RFP:

-   LOI   .-.. --- ..
-   RFP   .-. ..-. .--.

Give it a try. I trust you'll find it easier than the data company's CEO's attempt to line up three separate proposals.

8

Do I Need an Option to Renew?

For many business owners, planning is common. For sales or revenue forecasting, hiring or benchmarking, a one-year, three-year or even a five-year plan is not unusual. Because projections, growth, and productivity lead to an inevitable staff increase, prudent business owners factor future growth into their space to accommodate such expansions. However, some business owners overlook the importance of planning for future growth in their lease document.

A growing business, let's call them the represent yourself company (RYC), made it through a recession with its customer base intact and anticipated future growth. So RYC hit the market calling every for lease property sign searching for the right office that could handle their sprawling space needs. RYC signed a five-year lease for double the space in a Class A property within a submarket that saw vacancies rise and rental rates plummet during the recession. RYC received a great deal, and the Class A space provided tremendous value and accommodations. Soon, RYC's brand identity elevated and their customer base recognized and esteemed RYC's new Class A corporate address. After all, the property was located in a key submarket with a who's who of Fortune 500 companies.

Their marketing materials not only contained the new office address but also prominently featured the building on the front of the corporate brochure. In fact, RYC incorporated the building into their newly redesigned company logo. Employees enjoyed the property's amenities including the cafeteria, gym, free covered parking, and the ease of access which their space provided given its proximity to the major highways. RYC's business was booming as their new office perfectly fit their projections, mission, and vision for the firm. RYC could not be more pleased with their office as the lease years swiftly passed by. But six months prior to their lease expiration, RYC received a letter from their landlord.

> "Dear President of RYC:
>
> It has been a pleasure to service your office space needs at Class A Property over the last four and a half years. RYC has been a model tenant.
>
> Please be advised, that due to an expansion option of the large Fortune 500 company located on the floor above RYC's space, we cannot extend an opportunity to renew your lease.
>
> Unfortunately, we have no other vacant space at the property. Therefore, as the current lease expires on December 31, RYC will need to vacate and surrender the premises to the landlord by the expiration date or be subject to the holdover provision of the lease.
>
> Should you have any questions, please do not hesitate to contact us. We wish you continued success.
>
> Sincerely,
> The Landlord"

In other words, RYC must vacate their office by the end of the lease, or face paying double rent plus any damages incurred by the landlord should RYC hold over and jeopardize the landlord's deal with the

Fortune 500 company. Multiple calls and meetings with the landlord did not change the fact that RYC needed to vacate their beloved space within six months.

Years of brand identity, employee satisfaction, and customer association with RYC's office space were now chaotically turned upside down. Instead of finalizing the end-of-year budgets, setting future sales forecasts, and planning year-end holiday parties and vacations, RYC will need to painstakingly undertake locating a new office and moving by the year's end. The difficulties include downtime, lost sales, relocation cost, new marketing materials expenditures and brand identity, diminished employee efficiency, unknown future base rent expenses, explanations to customers why they are moving, and general uncertainty.

As if RYC's troubles were not challenging enough, five years of rent growth and absorption had taken place within the submarket. For Class A space of similar quality in the same submarket today, RYC can expect a rent increase of over 30 percent annually. And RYC has no choice but to pay the increase as their customers and employees have come to value and expect a Class A office environment. Settling for less may send the message the firm is moving in a downward direction resulting in lost business and poor employee morale. RYC's CEO is an Overwhelmed Business Owner.

Does this sound like an impossible scenario? Unfortunately, too many business owners fail to recognize the importance of controlling the future of their leasehold space. The excitement of a new office, the daily task of conducting business, and the far-reaching trust of a leasing agent can lead to a tenant not considering a future renewal—assuming it will all work out.

For RYC, one simple negotiated clause in the lease would have assured their landlord could not kick them out. One common provision often given freely by landlords when asked could have prevented six months of disruption for RYC. The provision is called an "Option to

Renew." Even the large Fortune 500 company would have to look for space elsewhere if RYC had an option to renew in their lease. An option to renew provision permits the tenant to renew his lease based on the negotiated conditions of the provision.

> An option to renew provision permits the tenant to renew his lease

Jason visited Mike's office to review the recently prepared RFP for the three properties under consideration.

As Jason sat in Mike's office, he asked, "How's your wife doing?"

"She's great, thanks for asking," answered Mike with a smile and gazing out the window as if picturing his next statement. "Last night in our Lamaze class, we spent the whole time expressing our fears. It turns out; all the dads-to-be voiced more fears than the moms-to-be."

"You and your wife will do great."

"Tomorrow night, we get to learn the breathing techniques."

"Oh, I remember those days," said Jason with a smile. "Truthfully, when my children were born, I applied the breathing techniques more than my wife." The two shared a good laugh and a few more Lamaze stories.

Mike then pulled out the RFP Jason emailed him earlier in the day. "Jason, I'm sure it's important because you included it in all three requests for proposal drafts, but what's an option to renew?" inquired Mike as he reviewed the RFPs.

"An option to renew is a lease provision stipulating the tenant has the absolute and complete right and privilege to renew the lease and stay in the space."

"Sounds ideal. How does this work?"

Jason answered, "A typical option to renew provision will contain these three basic conditions:

- Prior written notice period necessary for the tenant to exercise the option (usually six to twelve months before expiration of the lease)
- The renewal period (typically three to five years from the termination date)
- The base rental rate during the renewal period (most landlords offer the then prevailing fair market rate)"

"That's a lot to absorb," retorted Mike. "I'm sure we'll be here a while, but can you explain each condition?"

"Sure," answered Jason and he gave the following explanation:

Prior Written Notice Period

"First, the prior written notice period sets a 'not to surpass' date for when a tenant must notify the landlord in writing of their exercising the option to renew in accordance with the lease."

"I see in the RFP you state a six months' prior written notice period. When would we need to give notice?"

"If the lease expires December 31 with a six months' prior written notice provision, the landlord would need to receive the tenant's written letter by no later than June 30," answered Jason.

"How do I notice the landlord? Can I send him an email or call the landlord?" asked an interested Mike.

"The notice provision of the lease will stipulate the landlord's address and the method for sending the notice—usually overnight mail by a nationally recognized carrier or certified mail by the US Post Office," replied Jason.

"Why six months' notice, can it be longer or shorter?"

"Excellent question," answered Jason. "A good method to settle this is to simply ask the question, 'Were I not to renew the lease, how long would it take for my company to relocate?' I chose six months because that's the time we'll need to either renew or sign a lease elsewhere to move." (Please visit chapter 5 for a further discussion on when to start looking for space).

Jason continued to explain, "Occasionally, the option to renew language may dictate the earliest the option can be exercised; for instance, no earlier than twelve months and no later than six months."

"Why?"

"The base rental rate will most likely be computed based on the prevailing fair market rate, which is a look ahead to where rental rates will be when the lease expires. We'll discuss this shortly," returned Jason sensing another question from Mike. "The farther away the option to renew is exercised from the eventual lease expiration; the less accurate the base rental rate estimate will be for the renewal period."

As usual, Mike wanted to know, "Is this bad or good for a tenant?"

"Both. It works to both the benefit and detriment of landlord and tenant," replied Jason.

"Really? How so?"

"In a downward market where rates are dropping, too long a notice period will hurt the tenant as they may leave dollars on the table by settling on a rental rate nine to twelve months too early. Perhaps the rate would have dropped further during that period. On the other hand, in an upward market where rates are increasing, landlords may leave dollars on the table by settling on a rental rate too soon," answered Jason to which Mike replied, "Got it."

Renewal Period

"Second, the renewal period sets forth how many years the lease will be extended. The renewal period will delineate the new expiration date," added Jason.

"How many years will the renewal be?"

"The renewal period can vary, but it usually matches the period of the initial lease term. A savvy tenant advisor may also push for a variable renewal term," answered Jason.

"What does that mean?"

"In other words, at the tenant's choice, the renewal period may be for one year or up to five years," answered Jason who added a word of caution, "This is not too common, and landlords are not very receptive to this concept. But it doesn't hurt to ask."

Base Rental Rate

"We briefly touched the last condition, the base rental rate section of the option to renew. This section is usually the most contested and heavily negotiated," continued Jason.

"How exactly will a tenant and landlord agree to what the rent will be five years down the road?" asked a puzzled Mike.

"The base rent for an option to renew is based upon the prevailing fair market rate, or FMR for short, at the time the option to renew is exercised. Most landlords will seek to capitalize on increasing future rents while tenants will seek to protect themselves from increasing rents," answered Jason.

"What if a tenant and landlord can't agree on the FM, uh, FM, radio thing—the same station?" asked Mike making the most of his blunder.

"Impressive recovery," answered Jason. "If the landlord and tenant are not *in tune* with the FMR, a sometimes overly complicated system known as 'Baseball Arbitration' or similar method can be used to estimate the FMR," answered Jason.

Now I'm totally lost, thought Mike, but his expression spoke volumes to Jason.

Anticipating Mike's next question, Jason added, "Baseball arbitration sets forth the guidelines for estimating the fair market rate in the event tenant and landlord disagree on the FMR calling for an independent arbitrator to be involved. The arbitrator will determine whether the landlord's or the tenant's proposed rate is most reflective of market rates."

"Oh, I get it. Both the landlord and a tenant get a *swing* at the FMR, and the arbitrator decides who gets the hit," said Mike.

"Home run, Mike," answered Jason. "So, it behooves both parties to propose a reasonable rental rate and negotiate in good faith—though most tenants and landlords avoid ever heading to arbitration."

"Why not just continue the same rental rate increases or fix the rates during the renewal?" asked Mike.

"Except for retail leases, rarely will an option to renew include fixed adjustments to the existing rents," responded Jason, disappointing Mike. He continued, "Landlords typically request for the base rent to be the higher of what the tenant is currently paying or the FMR."

"Why would a tenant agree to this?"

"Obviously, this is a tremendous hedge for a landlord against deflation of rents and should not be accepted by tenants. I assure you, we won't agree to this," affirmed Jason. "Conversely, tenants should seek a base rent for the option to renew of the lesser of what the tenant is paying or the FMR."

"That sounds better," confirmed Mike.

"Mike, you can see why the determination of what the future rents will be is such a highly contested matter in a lease negotiation," stated Jason.

Mike nodded his head.

"However microscopic this one business point may seem, as it usually doesn't have a significant impact for years, it is always best to plan for an equitable future transaction and avoid troubles between a tenant and a landlord," said Jason.

"I agree," reiterated Mike.

"We'll consider additional option to renew provisions when we further negotiate the RFP," said Jason.

"Such as?"

"Well, what about concessions such as free rent and TI? In a full-service lease, what happens to the base year? What happens in the event of a sublease or assignment?" asked Jason raising concerns Mike would have never considered.

"I'm glad you are well-versed in these matters, Jason," stated an appreciative Mike as he thought of another question. "What if I plan on aggressively expanding or if I don't particularly like my space, should I care if I have an option to renew?"

Jason began to answer, "Mike, it's always…"

"What if the FMR is far above what I am prepared to pay, does an option to renew benefit me?" interrupted Mike as he snapped and pointed his fingers in one motion.

"Mike, the answer to your questions is an emphatic YES," answered Jason. "Leverage is tilted in the tenant's direction when an option to renew is at hand.

"Even if it's never exercised?"

> an option to
> renew assures
> you can stay
> in place

"Even if it's never exercised, an option to renew assures you can stay in place if you desire or use it as a stop gap if you need to stay due to market conditions," affirmed Jason. He continued, "It also provides a negotiating chip at renewal time for nothing prevents a tenant from negotiating with the landlord early before exercising the option to renew."

Mike Johnson didn't realize he had an option to renew in his lease until it was too late. By the time he engaged Jason Woods to represent him, the notice provision had expired. Should the software company desire to stay in the current space, it would be at the sole discretion and election of the landlord. Fortunately, Mike realized the importance of possessing an option to renew, thanks to his tenant advisor, and he was certain to have it included the RFP and in his future lease. Further, Jason secured favorable conditions within the option to renew provision assuring the software company could enjoy their new office long into the future.

A well-versed tenant advisor can be a vital help in negotiating the most favorable option to renew terms and conditions.

Who should have an option to renew in their lease? Every tenant.

9

Is a ROFO Dog Speak?

I'll never forget picking up an eight-week-old puppy with my two daughters. We drove early on a Saturday morning to Orlando, Florida to meet a dog breeder at a Cracker Barrel. Upon adopting the Goldendoodle puppy, which we aptly named Maple, my girls immediately wrapped their arms around the puppy and spoke to the dog with wide smiles and high-pitched voices. And the puppy responded with many tail wags and kisses. The dog speak continued for hours as we drove home with our new canine family member. Is this high-pitched dog speak known as ROFO? Does a ROFO have anything to do with dogs?

ROFO?

Do you remember the lunch conversation between Mike Johnson and Tony, the leasing agent? Apparently, the software company had a ROFO in the lease. Did this mean Mike and his programmers and engineers could bring their dogs to work? Why not cats?

Let's end the suspense; no, a ROFO is not dog speak. However, a ROFO can make a business owner nearly as happy as handling a new puppy.

"Jason, another provision I don't quite understand is the ROFO. Please tell me this doesn't deal with taking your dog to work?" asked Mike as he continued to review the RFP.

Right of First Offer

"It has nothing to do with dogs," answered Jason with a chuckle. "ROFO stands for a Right of First Offer. This provision requires the landlord to first offer available space within the building to you before offering the space to others."

Jason picked up on Mike's facial expression as he squinted his eyes and half nodded his head. Jason further elaborated, "In other words, it gives the tenant the first rights on available or future available space known as ROFO space. A ROFO is an excellent provision affording an opportunity for future growth, and along with an option to renew, should be included in the RFP."

"Thanks, Jason, I knew I wasn't close," responded Mike. "I've never heard of this provision until the leasing agent mentioned it at lunch. Will a ROFO really help the software company?"

"I often canvass properties either on behalf of clients or to prospect for new clients," said Jason. "I regularly find companies that have multiple offices throughout the property. Two spaces on the ground floor, one on the second, and another space on the fourth floor."

"That sounds terribly inefficient."

"This fractured office model is *highly* inefficient, costly, and disruptive to business. Each scattered office throughout the property requires separate and independent kitchen areas, reception areas, copy/fax rooms, storage rooms, IT closets, etc.," affirmed Jason.

"Sounds like a foolish business plan. How would I ever manage my employees and coordinate their efforts? Wouldn't all those standard areas be consolidated if the company had one space?" asked Mike.

"That's correct. The scattered office model could have been prevented if the company had a ROFO provision in their lease," added Jason proving his point. "A ROFO allows a business owner to grow the office systematically in an orderly fashion."

> A ROFO allows a business owner to grow the office

"If a ROFO is so beneficial, why doesn't every tenant have the provision in their lease?"

"Remember, the landlord prepares the lease," answered Jason. "A ROFO is not voluntarily offered by property owners and often resisted as the control of a vacant or future vacant space passes from the property owner to the tenant."

"Then who gets ROFO provisions in their lease?"

"Typically, only larger tenants possess this right," answered Jason. "And usually only tenants represented by a tenant advisor will even know to ask for this beneficial provision."

As Mike contemplated his next question, one of his engineers came into his office and said sarcastically, "Oh, *Mikey*, there's an Uncle Bob on the line for you." Mike looked at Jason in dismay. "He asked for Mikey and wanted to visit you as he's in town for the day."

"Uncle Bob?" questioned Mike. "I don't have an Uncle Bo-," Mike never finished the name when he looked at Jason and said, "You don't think that's…No! It can't be The Closer!"

"No way!" retorted a surprised Jason.

"Please tell long lost Uncle Bob that he'll have to leave a voice message for *Mikey*," said Mike.

"Jason, back to my favorite question: how does a ROFO work? What are the conditions?"

"The conditions of a ROFO will vary depending on each negotiated deal," answered Jason. Noting a hint of disappointment in Mike over the answer - he quickly added, "However, a typical landlord ROFO Notice will contain these provisions:

- Description of the ROFO space including suite number and square footage (typically the ROFO space will be limited to adjacent or contiguous space)
- The proposed base rental rate for the ROFO space (normally the then quoted rental rate at the building)
- The date the ROFO space is available for lease
- The proposed tenant improvements and additional incentives for leasing the ROFO space
- The time frame for a tenant to respond exercising its right to lease or not lease the ROFO space is also included in the notice.

The period is commonly ten days," finished Jason.

"So, if I understand this right—if I elect not to lease the space when my landlord serves me notice, then my right goes away?" wondered Mike.

"Not always. Right of First Offers can be presented on a one-time basis or an ongoing basis," responded Jason.

"OK, what's the difference?"

"A one-time ROFO will expire and no longer be valid should the tenant receive a ROFO Notice from the landlord and fail to take the space," explained Jason. "In an on-going ROFO, should the landlord provide a ROFO Notice and a tenant passes on leasing the space, the landlord will once again offer the space to the tenant in the future should the same space again become available."

"That works better. Let's be sure the ROFO in the RFP is an on-going one," stated Mike.

"Already included, Sir."

"You mentioned the notice period is commonly ten days. That's not a lot of time to decide," said a concerned Mike.

"I concur ten days is not ideal," said Jason. "However, you and I will often communicate regarding any expansion needs, and I will keep you abreast of the potential vacancies within the property," reassured Jason. "This extra insight will keep you from being surprised by a ROFO Notice and well prepared to act upon said notice."

"Are there any other mechanisms to grow your space during the term of the lease?" asked Mike taking notes once again.

"Fantastic question," said Jason. "In fact, there are a few more provisions, which you'll find in the RFP I prepared, that deal with this topic, such as a ROFR."

Right of First Refusal

"While similarly offering a tenant future growth opportunity as a ROFO, a Right of First Refusal (ROFR) provides additional leverage to a tenant," explained Jason.

"ROFO and ROFR, that can be confusing," admitted Mike as he wrote the acronym down.

"True, but they are significantly different," said a sympathetic Jason. "In a ROFR, when an adjacent space becomes available to lease, the landlord offers the space to the tenant only after receiving a bona fide third-party offer—that is an offer from another tenant."

"Remind me, the ROFO is offered based on the landlord's current market rates?" asked Mike.

"Correct, and the ROFR is offered based on the finalized negotiated terms and conditions with a third-party user," answered Jason.

"Can you elaborate the difference?"

"Of course; by the time the landlord offers you the space for lease in a ROFR, the landlord has previously marketed the space to others, toured the space, received offers, and negotiated an acceptable deal for the space with another prospect," related Jason. "At this point, when the landlord has a deal in hand with another company, he must slow down the process for ten days, risk losing the deal, and offer the space to you based on the provisions of the agreed upon deal."

"All right—so in a ROFO, as soon as the space is available, the landlord notifies the tenant?"

"Yes."

"And in a ROFR, the space can be available, but the landlord won't notify the tenant until there's an agreed proposal for the space?" questioned Mike seeking affirmation.

"You got it," attested Jason. "You can quickly perceive why landlords shy away from offering a ROFR as it could potentially endanger an ongoing transaction. Many deals have been negated due to an existing ROFR which leaves the burden on the landlord to maintain and track each ROFR right before leasing encumbered space."

"I see another provision in your RFP called 'Expansion Option.' Please explain," requested Mike.

Expansion Option

"Sure. Another vehicle to ensure your company has the future ability to grow when needed, is an expansion option," said Jason. "If a ROFR is not easily attainable from landlords, an Expansion Option is avoided by landlords like a plague, for a good reason."

"Why?" questioned Mike.

"An expansion option offers a business owner the right to lease contiguous space (that is space sharing a common wall) or any other space identified in the lease at any time at their sole discretion. The space in question is called expansion space," answered Jason.

"What's wrong with that? Sounds perfect for the tenant."

"Perfect for the tenant, yes," said Jason, "but not for the landlord. Think what that means—the landlord must make difficult choices regarding the expansion space. He has two options: 1) leave the expansion space vacant throughout the lease term waiting to see if the expansion option is ever exercised, or 2) lease the expansion space to others and be prepared to relocate the company occupying the space, should the expansion option be exercised."

"Now I understand. An expansion option freezes space for future use, which may or may not happen," acknowledged Mike. "The space might remain vacant indefinitely."

"That's why expansion options are extremely rare, and primarily, only larger companies occupying a significant portion of the building ever obtain such rights," reciprocated Jason. "In the late 2000's, as the economy tried to rebound from the Great Recession, several large companies such as law firms and financial institutions in depressed markets like the Miami Central Business District obtained expansion options in their lease. Almost a decade later, space was still vacant due to the encumbering nature of pending expansion options."

Mike and Jason concluded the discussion and their review of the RFP. Mike was positive the provisions requested in the RFP would provide the best protection for the software company.

A few days later, Mike Johnson finally received the ROFO Notice from Tony, the leasing agent for the space on the floor below his office. The letter read as follows:

"Dear Mr. Johnson:

Under Article 8, Right of First Offer, of the lease, the landlord is officially notifying you that ROFO space is available per the following conditions:

- ○ *The ROFO space is defined as Suite 350 and measures approximately 5,000 rentable square feet*
- ○ *The base rent shall be twenty dollars ($20.00) per rentable square foot NNN, plus twelve dollars ($12.00) per rentable square foot in OPEX. The base rent shall increase five (5%) percent per annum*
- ○ *The ROFO space shall be available within sixty days from the date of this notice*
- ○ *The ROFO space is being offered in "as is" condition.*

Please respond within ten (10) days to elect to lease or not to lease the ROFO space

Tenant elects to lease   *Tenant elects not to lease*
ROFO space   *ROFO space*

_____   _____

Please contact me with any questions or comments.
Sincerely,

Tony Di Proprietario
Leasing Agent for the Landlord"

Mike was well prepared to respond, given he and Jason already determined they could use less space in another location. Mike quickly signed the "Tenant elects not to lease the ROFO space" signature line and returned the document to a disappointed Tony.

Understanding the different mechanisms and provisions in which a business owner can expand their premises is key before committing to any lease. A favorable means of growing your space can provide for the use and enjoyment of your office space for future years. A reputable tenant advisor can secure the best provisions to ensure your company can expand when needed.

10

My Lease Has Radon Gas?

Mike Johnson, at the request of his tenant advisor, Jason Woods, read through his entire lease (recall he stopped reading at the base rental schedule found on the second page of the lease). Jason wanted Mike to become acclimated with the lease and the legal language as they were ready to forward the RFP.

"A customary lease contains many non-monetary provisions which can disrupt business owners," said Jason.

"Jason, I've come to perceive it's important to understand exactly what I am signing and binding the company to," returned Mike.

Though much of the lease was sleep inducing for a software engineer by trade, Mike propped up and took notice when he arrived at the Radon Gas Disclosure toward the end of the lease document. "Am I to invest in gas masks for all my employees?" questioned Mike. One of the many emergency voice messages he left for Jason came when he discovered the radon gas provision in his lease. "Jason, my lease has radon gas! Help!"

The next day, Jason visited Mike for a brief review of the lease and Mike's questions, especially the question about radon gas.

"Many provisions of a lease agreement are what I call boilerplate provisions," began Jason. "These are standard provisions common in every lease document. The Damages and Destruction clause, Subordination,

Attornment, Default, Landlord Remedies, and Eminent Domain are found in one form or fashion in most leases."

"Yes, I recall glancing over those paragraphs," said Mike.

Jason continued, "A lease may even contain a section in all caps whereby both parties, landlord and tenant, waive their right to a trial by jury."

"Why would anyone ever agree to waive their right to a trial by jury?"

"This provision keeps the landlord and tenant out of a long, drawn out, and costly court case. Arbitration or other means can handle any disputes," answered Jason. "Mike, I always advise my clients to have an experienced commercial real estate attorney review the lease, and I'm happy to recommend a few I've worked with over the years."

> **have an experienced commercial real estate attorney review the lease**

"After reading my lease, I think I concur."

"One boilerplate lease provision that may cause undue alarm is the radon gas section often found toward the end of the lease (perhaps for this reason)," said Jason.

"Yes, it was quite a shock to see that in my lease," answered Mike, "should I be concerned?"

Radon Gas Disclosure

"Mike, early in my real estate career, I too had no idea about radon gas," replied Jason as he recalled a story from his past. "Over twenty years ago, I was touring space on an upper floor of a high-rise office property with waterfront views. The property owner preemptively demolished all the tenant improvements on the floor to market a shell or white boxed space—a clean, wide open space with no walls inhibiting the ocean views."

"Upon exiting the elevator with the prospective tenant—a group of three to four executives—I spoke of the many property amenities and how the landlord's architect could quickly draft a test-fit space plan for the entire floor."

"You were the leasing agent then?" asked Mike following the story.

"That's right. I started in the business as a leasing agent working for a developer," answered Jason. "As with most well-trained leasing agents, I quickly led the tour to the window line to show off the beautiful ocean and city views. 'On a still morning as the sun rises, the bay looks like a sheet of glass,' I chimed in as we gazed out the window."

"I bet that space was expensive!" exclaimed Mike.

"Not back then," answered Jason and he returned to the story, "As we continued to admire the views and discuss the property, I noticed one executive was missing from the tour. I lost one."

"Where did he go?"

"I turned around and to my astonishment, had to look twice. In the center of the floor, I found the lost senior executive squatting holding a string in his right hand and his left hand scratching his chin. He was intently looking down at a marble attached to the end of the string." said Jason with a look of amazement as if the event were happening right there and then.

"Have you lost your marbles?"

"What on earth was he doing?" asked Mike.

"I wondered the same thing," said Jason. "I couldn't take the suspense any longer and excused myself from the group to make my way slowly to the man deep in his study. In the back of my mind, I wondered, *why am I the only one on the tour that finds this unusual?* The others acted as if this was normal and continued in the conversation taking in the views."

"Calmly and timidly, I asked the gentleman, 'Excuse me, sir, but I've never seen this before. What are you doing?' Mike, this is what came out of my mouth, but what I really wanted to ask if he had lost his marbles. 'I'm testing for radon gas,' he answered frankly still staring at the marble."

"Testing for radon gas?" stated a surprised Mike.

DON'T SIGN THE LEASE!

"Yep," affirmed Jason. "The executive then added, 'If radon gas were moving through the building, the waves would press up against the marble on the string, and the marble would sway like a pendulum.' Oh. Wow! I had no idea! At an early start in my career, I learned about radon gas."

"What about the marble? Did it swing?" asked a curious Mike.

"Thankfully, the marble did not sway but hung steady on the string. What a relief!"

"Jason, what is radon gas and why does my lease contain a radon gas provision?"

Jason removed his laptop from his backpack and placed it on Mike's desk. After starting it up and connecting to the Wi-Fi, he maneuvered to the Florida Health website about radon gas. "Mike, take a look at the following excerpt from the Florida Health website (www.florida-health.gov):

'The **Notification on Real Estate Documents** [Section **404.056(5)**, Florida Statutes (F.S.)] shall be provided "at time of, or prior to, contract for sale and purchase of any building or execution of a rental agreement." This Statute requires the following statement:

"RADON GAS: Radon is a naturally occurring radioactive gas that, when it has accumulated in a building in sufficient quantities, may present health risks to persons who are exposed to it over time. Levels of radon that exceed federal and state guidelines have been found in buildings in Florida. Additional information regarding radon and radon testing may be obtained from your county health department."

"The EPA provides further information regarding Radon Gas, its effects, and how to test for it on its website (www.epa.gov)," explained

Jason. "The EPA's website contains an interesting map of the United States broken down by county with general Radon Gas zones. It's quite fascinating."

"I'll need to look up my townhome to see where I stand on that map," said Mike. He asked, "Then, radon gas occurs naturally and can be found anywhere in the United States including this area?"

"Yes," confirmed Jason. "The naturally occurring gas found in soil is diluted in an outdoor environment with the fresh air and rarely provides much risk. However, in a building, cracks in the foundation can potentially release radon gas 'trapping' the gas indoors and significantly increasing the risk."

"And every lease has this Radon Gas Disclosure?" asked Mike.

"Correct. Therefore…"

"So, my lease doesn't have radon gas!" exclaimed Mike relieved he wouldn't need gas masks for the office.

"No, your lease or property most likely does not contain radon gas," said Jason providing much-needed consolation to Mike. "But in this state, every lease must contain the Radon Gas Disclosure statement. Each state may have a different requirement."

Not until Mike spoke with his tenant advisor was he put at ease regarding the boilerplate provision. And he was not surprised when his future lease document also contained the same provision, word for word.

Any business owner concerned about radon gas should ask the property owner if the building has ever been tested for it. And be sure to confirm if the test included more than just a marble on a string. Before signing a contract would be an ideal time to request a radon gas test since the contract, either for lease or purchase, will contain the Radon Gas Disclosure. Please visit either website (www.floridahealth.gov or www.epa.gov) referenced in this chapter for further information on radon gas.

Part One Conclusion: Mike Johnson Signs a New Lease

Jason Woods forwarded the customized RFP for the software company to each of the three properties. The responses came in at the appointed time set forth by Jason. With each response, he provided a deal cost comparison which lined up each business point of the three offers.

Using the deal cost comparison sheet allowed Mike to track the progress as they made counteroffers and received revised offers from the landlords. The RFP and deal cost comparison analysis prepared by Jason streamlined the process of objectively defining the best value for the software company. During this time, the test fits were also completed and priced out as the cost of the tenant improvements were a key component to the deal cost comparison analysis.

With several rounds of negotiations behind them, Mike made a well-contemplated, informed, and confident decision. He selected Space Option C for the software company's future home. Though not the low-cost leader, the efficiency of Space Option C allowed for the best value when comparing the rent-per-employee. Mike decided the rent-per-employee was the best comparison metric for the software company. Space Option C also provided a turnkey build-out allowing for Mike to design his ideal layout while protecting the software company from any expenses related to the tenant improvements. Additionally, Jason negotiated favorable provisions in the proposal relating to future growth or contraction providing key flexibility to the software company.

The final proposal, based on the RFP, was prepared and ready for signature. Next, Mike needed to present his findings and recommendations to the software company's board of directors for approval before signing the proposal.

Just a few months earlier, Mike was an Overwhelmed Business Owner faced with the daunting and intimidating task of making a real estate decision about the software company's lease (he knew nothing of commercial real estate and had never read his lease). He would then have to present his logic behind that decision to the board of directors—with his job on the line! But thanks to his tenant advisor, Jason Woods, he looked forward to making his case to the board of directors to relocate the office to Space Option C. With a sense of boldness knowing he was making a triumphant decision for the software company, he prepared the slide deck for the board of directors. In fact, Mike already had the entire presentation in hand from Jason. He simply assembled Jason's work.

The presentation comprised the following sections:

- Section One – Tenant Representation Agreement
- Section Two – Kick-Off Checklist
- Section Three – Pre-Tour Phase
- Section Four – Office Market Overview
- Section Five – Property Tour Book
- Section Six – RFP Review and Landlord LOI Responses
- Section Seven – Deal Cost Comparison
- Section Eight – Test-Fit Space Plan and TI Cost Analysis
- Section Nine – Space Option C Recommendation
- Section Ten – Construction Timeline and Moving Plan

The day of the board meeting finally arrived. The meeting was in the conference room at the software company's office. Several board members entered the room with a skeptical bent having been previously briefed that Mike would recommend relocating the office. These board members believed the current office and building perfectly suited the software company's office requirement.

Mike started the presentation and walked through the slide deck he and Jason prepared. After each section, Mike asked, "Any questions thus far?"

"No, please continue," affirmed a different board member each time impressed with the presentation and Mike's fortitude as he confidently outlined his case to relocate the office.

By the time he concluded the presentation, most board members were in agreement with Mike to relocate the office. Only one leery board member remained, Mr. Curmudgeon. "Mike, you certainly outlined a powerful case to relocate the office, and saving 50 percent on rent is ideal," said Mr. Curmudgeon complimenting Mike before presenting his doubt. "But I question taking substantially less space. What happens if we outperform our growth models—we'll be stuck in too small of space?"

"Actually, Mr. Curmudgeon, our tenant advisor, Jason Woods, negotiated a favorable expansion option in the deal. If we need more space, the landlord will need to provide it," quickly responded a resolute Mike.

"How can you be certain the move won't cost the software company money in tenant improvement overruns," continued Mr. Curmudgeon who apparently didn't like change. "Isn't it better to stay put?"

"Mr. Curmudgeon, that was one of my main concerns. But Jason Woods negotiated a turnkey build-out for us. Problem solved," answered Mike.

"How so?"

"In a turnkey build-out, the landlord covers the tenant improvement costs in accordance with the plans and specifications agreed upon. The lease will contain the plan and all the details necessary to protect us," responded Mike. He respectfully added, "We covered that during Section Eight of the presentation."

"Well, uh," began Mr. Curmudgeon struggling to come up with any more roadblocks, "what if the space isn't delivered in time? Huh? We don't want to face holdover rent."

"Not to worry, Mr. Curmudgeon," said Mike. "Recall Section Ten: Construction Timeline and Moving Plan?" Mike brought up on the screen Section Ten for Mr. Curmudgeon's second look. "We have more than adequate time allotted for the move. In fact, we have an extra thirty days to spare in case of any unforeseen delays."

This time, Mr. Curmudgeon only responded with silence and a nod of his head.

"Any other questions?" asked Mike gazing around the conference room table ready to squash any further naysayers like a kid playing whack a mole. No more comments or questions came his way.

Within a few minutes, the board of directors unanimously approved the deal to relocate the software company's office to Space Option C.

"Well done, Mike," said Mr. Curmudgeon shaking Mike's hand as he left the conference room. All the other board members followed suit.

With six months remaining before the lease expiration, Mike signed the lease agreement for ten thousand rentable square feet at Space Option C. Mike didn't sign just a lease. *He signed a vehicle of prosperity for his firm, a conduit to further promote his vision and values for his business.*

Following the plan set by Jason Woods, Mike could return to his daily duties at the software company. Jason even remained in contact with Mike and the new landlord of Space Option C during the construction phase. With only a few weeks before the move, Jason's involvement allowed Mike to disconnect from the office to enjoy time with his wife and their newborn girls (yes, they had twins).

The software company moved into their newly completed Class A office space right on schedule. Mike was profusely satisfied with the final design and look of the office. He was eager to start the new year in a space that embodied his outlook for the firm and his role. A year ago, Mike was overwhelmed by Tony Di Proprietario who spoke of real estate phrases Mike didn't understand and had never heard of. Just one year earlier, the pressure of the new promotion to president of the software company heated up sevenfold as he faced the pending lease without a clue how to proceed. One year later, thanks to the efforts of his tenant advisor and now friend, Jason Woods, he sat in his new office with tremendous jubilee and the respect of his board of directors. Mike Johnson is a Triumphant Business Owner.

Following the move, the board of directors gathered in Mike's new office. This time, they shook hands to congratulate Mike on the new address, and to inform him of the new substantial increase to his salary.

"Mike, the software company is in great hands. You did a wonderful job. The space looks great," affirmed Mr. Curmudgeon.

"Thank you for your vote of confidence and trust, Mr. Curmudgeon."

"And oh, please forward me Jason Woods' contact info," said Mr. Curmudgeon. "I'd like to refer him to a few colleagues who need his help."

Mike gladly complied.

PART TWO

Avoiding Pitfalls

The Continued Sayings of Jason Woods

11

Pitfall One – The Uncooperative Landlord

If I could shout the title of this first pitfall from the top of a mountain or hi-rise rooftop with a megaphone in hand, I would. "Run, run from a landlord who will not work with your tenant advisor!" In the words of J.R.R. Tolkien's Gandalf character in *The Lord of the Rings*, "Fly, you fools!" If you are not familiar with this line, Gandalf, the wizard was battling a Balrog, a fire-breathing demon, and he wanted to warn his companions to flee from danger. Not that I want to unnecessarily compare any landlord to a fire-wielding agent from the underworld, but a landlord who is unwilling to work with a tenant advisor will likely burn a business owner.

I will assume you've already read the earlier chapters of this book and appreciate the value of a knowledgeable tenant advisor acting as your advocate, representing YOUR best interest in a real estate transaction. Consider that most landlords find it profitable and necessary to hire a broker to represent their best interest. Why shouldn't you likewise have representation?

The landlord broker, often called a leasing agent, is in a fiduciary relationship with the landlord to represent the landlord to his fullest ability and purpose. A fiduciary relationship means the broker is under a contractual obligation of trust to work for the best interest of his client, in this case, the landlord. Though very professional and courteous, the leasing agent's loyalty lies with the landlord. He or she works for the landlord, *not* the tenant. The landlord's representative, whether a broker or an in-house employee, is not a neutral participant in your real estate dealings and negotiations.

> **The landlord's leasing agent is not looking to negotiate the best deal for YOU.**

The landlord's leasing agent is not looking to negotiate the best deal for YOU. He is under contractual obligation to negotiate the best deal *for* the landlord. The landlord's proposal will not include the best terms and conditions for YOU. The landlord's attorney will not prepare a lease with YOUR protection in mind.

There is a proverb in the Bible that states, "Plans are established by counsel; by wise guidance wage war (Proverbs 20:18, ESV)."

When a business owner negotiates directly with the leasing agent without a tenant advisor, it's like going into battle against the landlord without wise guidance. It's the equivalent of a defendant choosing to have the prosecuting attorney represent him in court—an unthinkable event!

Business Owner X of a local non-profit organization hired a tenant advisor to represent his corporate office's relocation. After the pre-tour phase, the tenant advisor and business owner determined five thousand rentable square feet would be ideal, and they chose five properties to tour in a specific submarket from a broad list of vacant spaces. The tour was scheduled, and at last, they set out to tour one Friday morning.

Unfortunately, after touring the first four properties, Business Owner X received an urgent call to return to the office, and they had to cancel the tour for the fifth and last property. *What a shame,* thought the business owner, *the last property seemed to fit the best based on the floor plan and brochure.* Since his tenant advisor was leaving the next day for a two-week trip out of the country, the situation became more frustrating.

The leasing agent for the fifth property was disappointed when he received the call from the tenant advisor to postpone the tour for at least two weeks. He learned the tenant touring was Business Owner X of a local non-profit organization, and his landlord client highly desired to lease their largest vacancy to them. So, the leasing agent called Business Owner X later that afternoon and invited him to tour the space. Business Owner X reluctantly accepted the invitation as the property was on the way home, and they met after-hours on Friday.

The layout was ideal, the residual value of the improvements matched exactly what Business Owner X needed. With a few exceptions, such as new kitchen cabinets, subdividing a large conference room into two offices, and changing the carpet and paint to match the organization's color schemes, the space seemed perfect.

The leasing agent for the fifth property worked all weekend with his landlord to prepare a proposal for the space. By Monday morning, he hand-delivered the proposal to Business Owner X with a deadline of five days to respond. The proposal for the fifth property contained these business points:

- Space: Suite 500 measuring 5,017 rentable square feet
- Term: Ten years
- Rate: Thirty-six dollars per rentable square foot (the quoted rate)
- Increases: Base rent to increase five percent per year
- Free Rent: None
- TI: None. Tenant to pay for any tenant improvements and lease the premises in "as is" condition
- Security Deposit: Four months' deposit plus a personal guarantee
- Brokers: None, except the landlord's broker

The leasing agent promptly called the next day to receive an update on the LOI. Business Owner X replied, "Thank you for your time to tour the space last week and for sending me the proposal. But please recall that my broker is out of town for two weeks at which time he'll provide our counteroffer."

"Oh, well, Mr. Business Owner X, I worked all weekend with the landlord to prepare the *best* possible proposal for your company," answered the leasing agent. "And I assure you that you can negotiate a better deal without your broker. If you include him in the deal, we'll have to raise the offer to compensate for his fee."

Surprised, Business Owner X responded, "Listen, those details are between you and my broker, but I mentioned early on we were working with a broker. And besides, he's performed a lot of work for us already, and I prefer to work with him."

"I understand, Mr. Business Owner X, but my landlord will not recognize your broker. Now that we've toured the space and sent you a proposal, it's too late to include your broker," insisted the leasing agent openly nervous about the conversation. "Also, we have two other proposals out for the space at better deals, so the space won't be on the market when your broker returns to town. We really gave you the best offer, much better than what we would have given your broker. I suggest you sign the proposal ASAP to lock up the space. The space won't be available much longer."

Does this sound familiar? A high-pressure pitch to secure a lease. A landlord unwilling to work with your tenant advisor. Let's break down the leasing agent's argument.

First, the fact the leasing agent for the fifth property knowingly went around the tenant advisor to tour space with Business Owner X is a poor start and a sign of dubious intentions.

Second, is the leasing agent's claim that he's given the "best possible proposal" true? The proposal echoed the leasing agent's quoted terms and conditions for the property. With no negotiations, this is the best deal? Really? The quoted rate, a lengthy lease term, no tenant improvements, no free rent, a high security deposit, and a personal guarantee; quite a great deal for the *landlord*, not the tenant. Besides, without the tenant advisor's involvement, how does Business Owner X know if he's even getting a market deal, much less a good deal? Will other properties offer a shorter lease term, more tenant improvements, a lower rental rate, and a lower deposit?

Third, the leasing agent claims, "I assure you that you can negotiate a better deal without your broker." Again, really? At the outset, one can discern the "deal" is missing many key provisions of utmost importance to Business Owner X. Where is the option to renew? Where will his employees park? How will the property accommodate future growth? Will he have the right to sublease or assign the lease? I could continue with the list of missing provisions the landlord doesn't offer which a business owner must address before finalizing any negotiations. The RFP the tenant advisor prepares will address many required provisions should any proposal be considered.

Fourth, the leasing agent claims if the tenant advisor is included in the deal, "we'll have to raise the offer to compensate for his fee." Is this accurate? It is true the landlord would have to compensate the tenant advisor based on the total base rental. That is industry standards. But to say he would have to raise the offer due to a tenant advisor's involvement is not necessarily true. Any sophisticated and knowledgeable landlord forecasts leasing assumptions annually for the budget. Typically, this occurs in the last few months of the preceding calendar year. Brokerage fees for both the landlord's and tenant's broker are considered during the forecasts of future income and leases. So, to state the landlord will need to raise the offer to pay the tenant advisor is stretching the truth.

What is more accurate, is that a typical listing agreement allows the landlord's broker, the leasing agent, to be compensated more, up to double, if a tenant advisor is not involved. So, the party that stands to lose the most if a tenant advisor is involved is the leasing agent, not the landlord. The leasing agent is highly motivated to sign direct deals as he earns a higher commission.

> **the tenant advisor preserves the integrity of the leasing process**

Most landlords prefer to work with a tenant advisor as the tenant advisor preserves the integrity of the leasing process and negotiations proceed smoother through the use of the RFP. Signing a deal is an easier task when a tenant advisor is collaboratively working with the tenant and the landlord to protect and negotiate the best deal for his client.

Fifth, the leasing agent claims the space will not be available for lease if Business Owner X awaits the return of his broker. He must sign the proposal ASAP. Is that so? The tenant advisor had already informed the business owner the fifth property had been vacant for over eight months. Given the market update provided by his tenant advisor which included all the vacant space in the market, this claim seems to carry no weight.

Here's my MEGAPHONE: The only winner in a negotiation where the landlord refuses to work with your tenant advisor is the landlord. *Run, run, RUN!*

Head for the hills!

Business Owner X was wise enough not to fall for the high-pressure sales pitch of the leasing agent for the fifth property and waited for his tenant advisor to return. After the delivery of the RFP's, the eventual proposal delivered by the fifth property included stipulations far more favorable than the "best deal" the leasing agent initially offered. Business Owner X came to learn all the properties on the short list included reduced rents (not the quoted rent) with 3 percent increases (versus 5 percent) and free rent (instead of none). All the properties, including the fifth property, offered a five-year term (not ten years) and at least twenty dollars per rentable square foot in tenant improvements (not 'as is'). All the properties offered key provisions such as an option to renew, a ROFO, the right to sublease and a termination option—conditions not offered initially by the leasing agent of the fifth property.

The sour start by the leasing agent trying to take advantage of the non-profit organization and negotiate the best deal for his landlord dampened Business Owner X's interest in the fifth property. The non-profit organization signed a lease at one of the other properties under consideration. Had Business Owner X fallen for the leasing agent's tactics, he would have been an Overwhelmed Business Owner burned with an expensive lease for the next ten years with little protection for his organization. But as wisdom prevailed, Business Owner X signed a conduit for the promotion and success of his non-profit organization leading him to be a Triumphant Business Owner.

Again, avoid the pitfall of signing a lease with a landlord who will not work with your tenant advisor, either for a new lease or renewal. Don't expect an uncooperative landlord during the negotiation phase to suddenly become a cooperative landlord once your business is lease locked. Please don't sign the lease provided by a landlord unwilling to work with your tenant advisor. That tale will lead to the making of an Overwhelmed Business Owner.

12

Pitfall Two - Never Sign a Personal Guarantee

The search for an office space can often be an exciting time for business owners. The right office can move a company into an unchartered success.

New Company ABC, which incorporated a few months earlier, received a small business loan setting the stage to open its first office. The business owner of New Company ABC wasted no time searching the desired neighborhood for the office location, calling every for lease sign he could find. Oddly enough, no one called back for days. At last, one landlord returned the call and set up a tour.

The space seemed to work well for New Company ABC, and the business owner even had an amicable experience with the leasing agent while negotiating the simple proposal. The process proceeded smoothly. The landlord even offered to make the tenant improvements so that the space would be freshly painted and carpeted.

The lease quickly followed a few days later. Though the lease was a lengthy forty-five pages, the leasing agent assured New Company ABC that the lease was a standard document with all the important information located on the first two pages of the lease. With that in mind, New Company ABC signed all the required pages of the lease, including all the back pages which he did not read. After giving a check for two months' deposit and the first month's rent in advance, New Company ABC received a set of brass keys and moved in.

Everything went well, until six months into the five-year lease: the one and only client of New Company ABC announced it was closing its U.S. operations effective immediately. With the loss of their key account, New Company ABC could no longer afford the office space. *I'll contact the friendly leasing agent to see if I can get out of my lease,* thought the business owner of New Company ABC.

After a few failed attempts to reach the leasing agent, the business owner reached out to the property manager. A meeting was scheduled and much to the business owner's surprise, not only could he not get out of the lease, but he was personally liable to pay for all future rents in the lease.

"How could this be, the lease is signed in New Company ABC's name, not my name?" responded the horrified business owner.

"Well, the back of the lease contains an attachment which is a personal guarantee. You signed it giving the landlord rights to go after you if you default." What was this Overwhelmed Business Owner to do?

> **every business owner should read all the pages of his or her lease**

For starters, it should go without saying that every business owner should read all the pages of his or her lease, and have a real estate attorney review the lease as well. Secondly, no business owner should ever agree to sign a personal guarantee.

What is a personal guarantee? A simple online search can obtain many definitions of a personal guarantee. In summary, a personal guarantee is a written promise by the business owner to pay any outstanding debt or in our case rent, if the business defaults on its obligations under the lease. In simple terms, the business owner handles the fulfillment of the lease, not just the business entity.

No one ever believes their business will fail, but just look at past giant corporations such as Enron and Lehman Brothers as examples of what can potentially happen to a business. Having serious conversations with a landlord regarding securitizing the lease and carefully reading and understanding the default remedies available to the landlord are vital steps before signing the lease. Any business owner should always properly assess the business plan and potential income with an eye to the affordability of the lease before signing any lease.

Please don't misunderstand my comment "a business owner should never agree to sign a personal guarantee" to mean I promote businesses and individuals to ignore a moral obligation to abide by the written contract. No, far from this; I strive to live by Jesus Christ's command, "Let what you say be simply 'Yes' or 'No; (Matthew 5:37, ESV)." Not the case. But several more equitable alternatives exist for securitizing a lease—alternatives which can limit the landlord's financial exposure while not placing a business owner under the duress of personally losing everything because of the personal guarantee (leading to an OBO).

"I should have never signed the lease."

Alternatives to a Personal Guarantee

With New Company ABC only having one key client, it would have been more prudent to sign a lease for a lesser term of one or two years instead of five years. This would have limited the rent exposure and risk for both tenant and landlord eliminating the need for a personal guarantee. New Company ABC could have leased the space in "as is" condition to avoid signing a personal guarantee. The lower out-of-pocket costs for the landlord would have limited the need to securitize the lease beyond a customary security deposit. It is better to deal with stained or worn carpet than to agree to be personally liable for the lease. Perhaps New Company ABC could have offered to pay an additional month of security deposit to avoid the personal guarantee.

Another option, though less desirable, is to limit the guarantee amount. Instead of personally guaranteeing the entire lease, a fixed amount such as the cost of the tenant improvements or one year's worth of rent could have been agreed to—which could burn off after faithful payment of rent.

A personal guarantee is not the only means available to a landlord to safeguard a lease. What if the preferred building's landlord will not agree to waive the personal guarantee even after considering alternatives to limit the landlord's risk? Keep searching. Find a landlord who is more accustomed to leasing space to local, more entrepreneurial, or newly formed companies and thus is more attuned to their needs. A seasoned real estate advisor will guide you to properties matching your specific needs and circumstances.

New Company ABC eventually hired a tenant advisor who marketed and subleased the space to another firm, thereby enabling them to fulfill their rent obligation and avoid personally paying for the lease. Triumph!

13

Pitfall Three - Not Possessing a Termination Option

In our previous example, within the first year of signing a five-year lease, New Company ABC realized they had to close their office unexpectedly. Another vehicle that could have mitigated their damages is a termination option.

A termination option grants a tenant an escape provision (or get-out-of-jail card) during the lease term providing a key strategic advantage to a business owner. This tenant right defines the conditions when a tenant can legally, preemptively end the lease before the lease's defined expiration date. Let's take a look at the key features of a termination option.

Basic Conditions of a Termination Option

First, the lease will identify a time frame delineating when a tenant can exercise its right to terminate the lease. Usually, a termination option applies only after several years of the lease have elapsed. For example, in a ten-year lease, a termination option would typically apply after the sixtieth month of the lease. The first sixty months would be the fixed portion of the lease term, while the remaining sixty months would be subject to the tenant's ability to end the lease.

Second, the lease will address a prior written notice period for the termination option. When a tenant desires to exercise the termination option, how much notice should the tenant provide to the landlord of its intentions? Such a prior written notice period could be as little as ninety days for smaller leases to up to twelve months for larger leases. Both the time frame (when a termination can be exercised) and the prior written notice period are negotiable items in the proposal and/or lease.

Termination Fee

Up to this point, a termination option seems like a flawless win for a business owner. Who doesn't want the flexibility of walking away from the lease if necessary, for any reason? But we must pause and consider the cost associated with a termination option. Yes, there is a cost. I didn't say it was a get-out-of-jail *free* card. Landlords hesitate to offer termination options for multiple reasons including chiefly the lost capitalization value of a lease, thereby devaluing the property. The capitalization value (cap value) is the compounded value an investor is willing to pay for the net operating income of a property. A lease with a termination option is discounted significantly, if included at all, in the valuation of the property's income because the income stream is uncertain.

> **consider the cost associated with a termination option**

Therefore, when landlords agree to a termination option, there's a stiff price to pay by the tenant known as a termination fee. The termination fee is the fee the tenant must pay to the landlord if the tenant cancels the lease before the scheduled expiration date. The termination fee can consist of:

- Unamortized cost of the tenant improvements
- Unamortized cost of the commissions
- Unamortized cost of the free rent
- Interest on the unamortized cost
- Rent penalty of up to six months

While all the above costs may or may not be included in the fee, a typical termination fee will include a reimbursement of the landlord's out-of-pocket costs associated with the lease. These costs include the commissions to the brokers (both the tenant and landlord broker), the tenant improvements, and the free rent if any. Landlords often apply interest to these costs. Fortunately, the reimbursement of the landlord's out-of-pocket costs only applies to the remaining lease portion term or the cost yet to be amortized known as the unamortized cost. The landlord will take his out-of-pocket costs and spread them throughout the lease term. Therefore, if the tenant abruptly cancels the lease, not all the costs have been accounted for.

Notice the commission reimbursement not only includes the fee for your tenant advisor but also includes the fee for the landlord's advisor. In most termination fees, a tenant will reimburse the landlord for the commission of the landlord's broker, though a savvy tenant advisor may negotiate this out of the termination fee.

The rent penalty will vary per market and landlord. In a tenant-favorable market, the tenant can negotiate away the rent penalty, but otherwise, it will most likely fall between two to six months of the rent at the time of termination.

"If my termination option will cost me several thousand or hundreds of thousands of dollars, why bother asking for one?" That's a good question and a question Mike asked Jason during their lease negotiation.

The answer is that a termination option, even if expensive or if it's never exercised, offers valuable leverage to a business owner. Consider it a potential future bargaining chip. One never knows if and how it's used to a business owner's advantage.

I once worked with a CPA firm that signed a five-year lease renewal at the top of the rental rate market. The CPA firm negotiated a termination option which they could exercise at any time after the end of the third lease year. This CPA firm had occupied the same space for over ten years, and the property's location was unique, close to the business owner's home and known by his clientele; he wasn't going anywhere.

Fast forward to year three of the lease, and we were now in the midst of the Great Recession. Rental Rates dropped nearly 30 percent, and the CPA firm was now grossly paying above market rent for his space. What could he do?

Mr. CPA recalled he had negotiated a termination option in his last renewal. He called the landlord and threatened to cancel the lease if the landlord did not lower his rent. Visualize a tenant coming to a landlord in mid-term of a lease to ask for a rent reduction. "The landlord didn't ask you for a rent increase when market rents outperformed your lease, so why should the landlord adjust your rent now that the market has tanked?" would be the standard line of most leasing agents. Ah, but a conversation with the landlord by a tenant possessing a right to terminate the lease will end in "yes, Sir" or "yes, Ma'am."

This was the case for the CPA firm. With the threat of another tenant loss in a depressed market, the landlord was willing to come to the table. Thanks to the leverage of the termination option, the landlord tore up the old lease, and offered a new deal at the current below market rental rates and included free rent plus new carpet and a fresh coat of paint.

Despite the high cost of having a contingency to terminate the lease early if needed, a termination option is advantageous and adds tremendous leverage to business owners. The termination fee cost provides enough pain so as not to be easily applied, but not so adverse that if needed, it cannot be used. Every termination option is unique, and each point depends on negotiations. A qualified tenant advisor will give input on the current market conditions and opportunities to negotiate each point of the termination option including the lowest possible termination fee.

14

Pitfall Four - Neglecting Early Access

Let's face it; lease agreements can be wordy, lengthy, and full of legal language. Reading a lease may not seem to be the most productive use of time. However tedious and boring it may be, reading and understanding the lease is non-negotiable. Not all lease provisions carry the same importance and impact. Many provisions are boilerplate, standard provisions found in all lease documents. Yet, landlords do not include many provisions most helpful to a tenant in a standard lease agreement, and a tenant must request and negotiate for their inclusion. After all, the lease agreement is prepared and provided by the landlord (and the landlord's attorneys) to protect the landlord.

One small and often forgotten provision is an early access right. Most business owners have not even heard of an early access provision, so what is it and why is it important? Allow the following illustration to explain:

> An expediting travel company ("ETC"), represented by Bob, the Closer of Bob the Closer Real Estate Company (they fell for his constant barrage of solicitations), signed a five-year lease for a full floor, nearly twenty thousand rentable square feet. As the property was a newly constructed office building, the space required

a full build-out and an expensive tenant improvement package. Given market conditions, the landlord agreed to perform and provide an allowance for the tenant improvements which would take an estimated six months.

Upon signing the lease, ETC informed their current landlord they will not be renewing the lease and will vacate their space in six months. You can probably gather where the story is heading. Unfortunately, the project was delayed due to the slow permitting process causing ETC to negotiate a pricey short-term lease extension with their current landlord. To make matters worse, the tenant improvement allowance was insufficient causing ETC to pay out-of-pocket for the tenant improvements. ETC attempted to reach out to their tenant broker, Bob, the Closer, for guidance, but they could not locate him and he didn't return their calls now that the lease was signed and his check cleared the bank! ETC was on their own.

One Friday afternoon, now the ninth month since the lease was signed, a letter was hand delivered to ETC by the new landlord stating the premises was ready for occupancy as the Certificate of Occupancy was just issued that morning by the City. In accordance with the lease, continued the letter, the lease for their new space will commence immediately.

ETC was in a bind. Though their new lease (and rent) had commenced, they were nowhere near occupying the space. First, they still owed rent on their short-term renewal for another two months caused by the delays in the tenant improvements of the new office. Second, due to the delay, they had not rescheduled the moving plans which included not only the moving of furniture, fixtures, and equipment (FFE) but also the installation of data and phone lines. While the movers only needed two weeks' notice to move the furniture, the phone company will need up to forty-five days to process the order and run new lines.

Rather than enjoying the common stresses of moving into a new office, ETC had the added burden of paying for both their current space and their new space which they can't even occupy for at least another forty-five days.

Could ETC have avoided this quagmire?

The answer is yes. ETC could have avoided the problematic start to their new lease if they had requested and negotiated an early access provision in their lease. ETC's broker, Bob, the Closer, should have requested this in the RFP, but as ETC came to find out, Bob, the Closer is a *professional income generator* (otherwise known as a P.I.G.) and not an advocate fighting for ETC's best interest.

Bob, the Closer, President of Bob the Closer Real Estate Company

Regrettably, Bob's chief concern since luring ETC as a client was to secure his commission. In fact, he negotiated the provisions of his commission agreement with more scrutiny and focus than he did ETC's deal, and thus paid no attention to the missing early access provision. Once his commission was paid, Bob was nowhere to be seen—he was off looking for his next prey.

What is an Early Access Provision?

Essentially, an early access provision grants a tenant exactly as it states, early access to the premises before the commencement of the lease. This early access right is to give the tenant the ability to set up their new space including moving the furniture, fixtures and equipment and installation of their data and phone lines before the commencement date. So, when the lease begins, the business owner has already moved in and is prepared to conduct business from day one thereby substantially diminishing downtime or loss of productivity.

The prior access time frame can vary depending on the size of the space and scope of work for the tenant improvements. I've negotiated anywhere from fourteen days to up to thirty days' prior access to the space before the lease begins. With an early access provision, the communication between tenant and landlord during the tenant improvement phase will be more frequent, so a tenant will not be surprised by a commencement letter from the landlord.

The provision need not say more than a few words: "Tenant shall be granted access to the premises thirty days prior to the commencement of the lease to move its FFE and installation of phone and data lines." One sentence would have saved ETC dollars and stress—thanks, Bob, the Closer!

While this is not a provision that will adversely affect a tenant during the duration of the lease term, an early access provision will ensure a favorable start to your new lease. Though some landlords will try to define further and limit the early access provision or decline to offer it altogether, a skilled tenant advisor, one truly working for the good of his client, will include this in any proposal and/or lease.

15

Pitfall Five - The Standard Sublease and Assignment Provision

Mr. Jones worked at a local insurance agency for many years writing policies and satisfying every customer. He was always the first agent in the office and the last one to leave. He was the best agent in the firm consistently securing more policies than any other agent.

One day, the main owner of the insurance agency, who rarely came to the office, took him out to lunch. "I'm considering retiring," started the owner, "would you like to purchase the insurance agency? I can't think of better hands to leave this business in than yours."

After much thought and number crunching, Mr. Jones secured a small business loan and gladly purchased the insurance agency. Driving into the office brought him a new personal and professional satisfaction as he finally owned the firm. "I've never been happier to get up in the morning and work each day," Mr. Jones daily contemplated.

And what a difference this newly found bliss made to the bottom line as Mr. Jones worked harder and solicited more business. Visiting chamber events, sponsoring local youth sports, speaking at the local Kiwanis club, and taking clients out to lunch soon produced more leads than the insurance agency could handle. Mr. Jones quickly faced the dilemma of either turning away customers or hiring more staff to accommodate the influx of new clients seeking insurance policies.

More staff will entail a larger office as we have maxed out our space, he supposed. He had already crammed as many desks as could fit within the office and his employees were grumbling at the poor work conditions. He was at a crossroad.

He decided, *we'll need to relocate and expand the office.* The next thought had the potential to dampen his enthusiasm for having just purchased the insurance agency, *Where's my lease?*

In the exuberance of purchasing and growing his firm, Mr. Jones had paid little or no attention to his lease. Embarrassingly, he telephoned the retired owner seeking the whereabouts of the lease agreement, only to learn it was stored in a lateral file in the back of the storage room, lowest drawer.

"This legal-sized document on blue back paper is my lease?" questioned Mr. Jones. As he read the many pages of fine print, it soon dawned on him that he did not understand what this document read. Sure, he could surmise the monthly rent on the first page (though the monthly figures didn't match his monthly billing from his landlord), and lease expiration date, which, to his surprise, was far down the road, but the rest of the document read like a poorly subtitled foreign film. He picked up a little here and there but couldn't follow the plot.

My lease doesn't run out for three years, but I need double the space. What do I do now? deliberated Mr. Jones.

In Mr. Jones's initial inspection of the lease, he didn't notice the sublease and assignment clause buried in the middle of the document. I have titled this pitfall, "The standard sublease and assignment provision" because most lease documents contain generic language governing a tenant's right to sublease or assign the lease. However, business owners should obviously make sure the lease contains this highly needed provision; and second, ensure the conditions are reasonably favorable.

Sublease and Assignment

What is a sublease and assignment clause? When a business owner no longer has the need for his space, the sublease and assignment provision grants the business owner the right to find a replacement tenant for the space. The potential reasons to sublease or assign your space are many and include, from a negative perspective, failed business dealings requiring the need to close the office. Or from a positive perspective, better than anticipated sales and growth may necessitate the need for a larger space as in Mr. Jones's case.

Perhaps the business is sold to a competitor or larger company which has an office across the street. Thus, the space and therefore the lease is no longer warranted. Whatever the cause, having a standard sublease and assignment clause is a *must* provision in a lease. A business owner should never sign a lease without this customary clause. Never.

> **a standard sublease and assignment clause is a must provision in a lease**

How do you know if your sublease and assignment provision contains favorable or reasonable stipulations? First, realize any sublease or assignment to another company *will be* subject to the landlord's approval. The property owner will want to know and approve any occupant in the building. Landlords can make exceptions to this rule—such as when an affiliated company or subsidiary takes over the business or if the business is transferred in a merger or sale.

The business owner must notify the landlord in writing of intentions to sublease or assign the space. A separate sublease or assignment agreement will be executed by the master tenant (known as the sublandlord) and the new tenant (known as the subtenant).

What's the difference between a sublease and an assignment? A few variations exist. A sublease permits the subtenant to occupy the space while paying rent to the sublandlord. The sublandlord—that is, the original tenant—continues to be liable for the obligations of the lease. In an assignment, the subtenant assumes the liability of the lease and pays rent directly to the landlord. The original tenant, or the master tenant, is officially removed from any liabilities or obligations of the lease—though some landlords will still require the master tenant to guarantee payment of rent.

Usually, a landlord consent form, provided by the landlord, will need to be executed by both the sublandlord and subtenant, and all signed documents (the sublease and/or assignment agreement plus the landlord consent form) will then be submitted to the landlord for approval. The approval process should be considered when setting the new subtenant's occupancy expectations.

Do landlords have the right to deny subleases or assignments once submitted? That question leads us to the second consideration, obtaining "reasonable" approval by the landlord.

Favorable Terms

I've seen several standard sublease and assignment provisions giving the landlord carte blanche approval over any sublease or assignment. In other words, the landlord can deny a sublease or assignment for any reason. Further, most standard provisions do not limit the time for the landlord to approve a sublease or assignment. The result of this overreaching approval by the landlord is in effect to negate the sublease and assignment right or at the very least to leave the tenant in a state of limbo for a lengthy time.

Imagine the stress and time waste of constantly submitting potential subtenants to the landlord for approval and waiting thirty or sixty days (or potentially indefinitely) only to find out the landlord denied the sublease for no apparent reason. Now compound that to a second and third time, all while you continue to pay rent on space you no longer need waiting for that happy day when the landlord responds favorably.

Therefore, a favorable sublease and assignment provision will contain language where the landlord's approval will not be unreasonably withheld, conditioned or delayed. That's it. Those few words referencing the landlord's reasonable approval and response time will iron out any potential wrinkles in subleasing or assigning the lease if needed in the future.

Why is this important? Consider a business purchase, for example, a national bank approaches a local investment firm occupying a prominent location on a major intersection in a Downtown market for a purchase. The bank has desired the prime Downtown location for years, and since the local investment firm possessed a coveted long-term lease, the national bank offered a far above market price to purchase the firm.

The business owner was elated with the offer and agreed to sell the business and all the assets on the balance sheet, including the leasehold interest. Not so fast—just one thing: the local investment firm's lease, though it contained a generic sublease and assignment provision, did not address mergers or acquisitions. Furthermore, in the event of a sublease or assignment, the landlord was not under any reasonable approval restriction or time constraints. Once this was revealed to the national bank, the purchase of the local investment firm was placed on hold and in jeopardy. Without an assignment of the lease for the space, there was no deal.

The investment firm left themselves in a vulnerable position by accepting the original sublease and assignment language in the lease. Though they possessed the sublease and assignment provision in the lease, the effect of the provision was negated due to the landlord's over-reaching approval and lack of time parameters for that approval. The national bank simply could not wait around hoping to have a landlord approval, so they moved on to their second choice. No sale.

I have only scratched the surface on favorable (or as with most leases, unfavorable) terms and conditions within a standard sublease and assignment provision. I could say much more regarding profit sharing, landlord recapture rights, the ability to lease to other tenants in the property, and marketing the sublease and assignment space. Though this sounds repetitive and much like a broken record, again, a reputable expert tenant advisor should offer relative guidance and suggestions on how to avoid the common pitfalls while negotiating the sublease and assignment provision.

16

Pitfall Six - The Relocation Clause

A financial firm in a high-rent district in the CBD leased a corner office on a high floor with unparalleled ocean views. The expansive window line provided plentiful natural light creating an amazing working environment. The entire space was designed with the phenomenal views in mind including full height glass walls in all the perimeter offices. The space was one of the premier office spaces in all the market, and the financial firm paid considerably above market rents to secure the lease. The price was not a deciding factor.

A year into the lease term, the landlord forwarded a notice to the financial firm that under the Relocation Clause in the lease, they would be relocated to a space of similar size on a lower floor within the next thirty days. All the provisions and conditions of the lease will continue in full force and effect including the rental rate. The lower floor space overlooked the parking garage. "What?" questioned the business owner. "How can this be? I didn't sign up for this!"

Does the landlord have the right to do this?

Most standard leases contain a relocation provision where the landlord may relocate a tenant to another space of similar size anywhere in the building at any time with reasonable notice. While the financial firm's example is an extreme scenario (from a high floor with ocean views to a lower floor with parking garage views), this scenario is not too far-fetched. Business owners put considerable time and energy in carefully selecting the best address and space in which to conduct business; any involuntary relocation during the lease can be disruptive and detrimental.

Most business owners sign lease agreements with the standard relocation provision intact. Sizeable tenants such as full floor users can negotiate out the relocation clause, but most tenants will have to live with the provision in their lease. Even so, that fact doesn't necessarily mean the business owner cannot soften the relocation provision to their benefit.

Relocation Questions

Business owners should consider several questions when reviewing a relocation clause in a lease. Who pays for the relocation cost including not only the furniture, fixtures and equipment, but also the letterhead, business cards, marketing materials, and phone and data lines? Please don't assume the landlord pays for the relocation cost. I've read leases where the landlord has the right at the tenant's expense to relocate the tenant. How much time is considered reasonable for a landlord to relocate a tenant? What does the landlord consider similar space within the building? How often should a tenant be relocated during a lease? What happens to the rent if the relocation space is larger or smaller? These and many more questions and considerations should be reckoned with by any business owner, regardless of size.

In our financial firm example, while not a large full floor tenant, the firm leased and paid for an extraordinary space. Given the unique corner office featuring ocean views, it would be reasonable and expected for the financial firm to have requested the relocation clause to be deleted in its entirety. What happens when a landlord refuses to delete the relocation clause?

Favorable Relocation Conditions

If the relocation clause has to stay, the next best step would be to negotiate more favorable conditions within the relocation clause itself. Beneficial conditions in a relocation clause can include:

- Relocation to a space featuring similar views
- Relocation to a space no lower than the current floor
- Relocation to take place only one time during the lease
- Landlord to improve the new space to match the tenant's current layout and improvements including finishes
- Landlord to pay for all reasonable relocation costs (i.e., marketing materials, furniture, letterhead, business cards, directory signs, phone, and data, etc.)
- Relocation not to occur during the last year of the lease or during a vital time of the year (as in tax season for an accounting firm)
- Tenant to have the right to terminate the lease in the event the relocation space is unacceptable
- Reasonable notice to be defined as no less than ninety days
- Relocation to a larger space will not increase the base rent

The above items show a sampling of the many ways business owners can protect themselves from being egregiously relocated during the lease term. Most landlords will accommodate reasonable changes to the relocation provision—if requested. Though most business owners will need to live with the relocation clause in their lease, given the high cost of relocating a tenant, landlords rarely exercise this right. Look for your tenant advisor to provide vital insight as to making the relocation clause more palatable and less likely the landlord will ever exercise this right in the lease.

17

Pitfall Seven - Hours of Operation — Overtime Charge

I've spent most of my career living in South Florida. If you are not familiar with South Florida, there's a reason many North Americans, especially retirees known as "snow birds," visit this region between November and April. Yes, the palm trees are nice, the ocean is beautiful, and the eclectic, cultural food is superb. But what truly draws millions of visitors to South Florida every year is the warm weather. While most of America is freezing and under snow during winter, we continue to golf, swim, grill, and ride our cars with the windows rolled down. Many tourists enjoy the tropical climate, yet it can also present challenges to business owners.

William, a mutual fund manager for a major New York financial firm, determined after years of planning to open his business and relocate to Miami (Florida has no state income tax!). His business would allow him to cater to his clients and pursue riskier yet potentially profitable investments. William opened Gana Mas, a hedge fund, and endeavored to find a small office in a Class A tower in the financial district. Shortly after signing the five-year lease, Gana Mas opened its doors on January 3.

William moved his residence into a hi-rise condo,

one block away from his new office so he could walk to work. The cool, crisp sixty-five degrees South Florida winter weather welcomed William early the morning of January 3, and with an eleven dollar latte in hand, he opened the doors at 8:30 a.m. The first day swiftly passed and he finally closed the office at 8 p.m. later that night. The long hours and fast pace did not let down, and before he realized it, first quarter results poured in. Gana Mas was an overwhelming success outpacing all the major indexes. Soon, the second quarter results were in with advancing revenues and results. The demands of the new firm and the long hours never diminished and William was routinely leaving the office after 8 p.m. He had many affluent clients in Europe, and he needed to be available to them later in the day.

At the start of the third quarter, now July 1, William questioned if the high pace and the protracted work day was impacting his health. *As the day's activities continue, I seem to be heating up,* he thought wiping sweat from his brow. Perhaps stress was gaining the upper hand, but it sure seemed warm in the office. The pattern continued. William noticed that toward the end of each day, beginning around 6 p.m., he perspired. *Is it me, or is the office sweltering hot?* As August approached, he could not take the heat any longer. The office was so hot and stuffy; he could no longer function as sweat drops would often fall on his paperwork, ruining his orders. He called the property manager.

"Ms. Property Manager, good day, I am William of Gana Mas, a hedge fund, in Suite 1000," began William.

"Good morning, William, how may I help you?" answered Lily, the property manager.

"I seem to have an air conditioning problem. I noticed that starting in July around 6 p.m., the air shuts off and very quickly the office is scorching hot," William mentioned and added, "I can't function after 6 p.m. and my business demands I stay open until 8 p.m."

"Thank you for letting me know, William," responded Lily. "I'll pull up your lease to see what the hours of operation are supposed to be."

Hours of operation, what's that all about? thought William.

"Ok, I have the lease in front of me," continued Lily. "Your lease states the landlord will provide HVAC on Mondays through Fridays from 8 a.m. to 6 p.m., and Saturdays from 8 a.m. to 1 p.m."

"Pardon me, but what is HVAC?" asked William.

"HVAC stands for heating, ventilation, and air conditioning," answered Lily. "The Hours of Operation section in your lease dictates the times the property will provide air conditioning to your space."

"But I was told I would have twenty-four hours, seven days a week access to my space," William quickly contested still not fulling grasping the concept of hours of operation.

"Why, yes, you have access to the space any time you'd like. It's just that the lease governs the times the landlord will pay to provide air conditioning to your space."

The conversation was on the fringe of derailing into a heated discussion. William wasn't getting acceptable answers and surmised he had a major problem on hand. "How is it then my office was very comfortable for most of this year? I think the landlord just recently started shutting off the air."

"Well, William, in our cooler months, the climate continues to be comfortable for several hours after the air is turned off. But in the summer months, it doesn't take long for the building to heat up," answered the property manager as politely as possible.

"But Lily, as I explained, I have clients in Europe, and my office must be open daily until 8 p.m.," protested William.

"If that's the case, you always have the option of paying for overtime air conditioning," countered the property manager.

"Paying for overtime air conditioning?" repeated William. "How much does that cost?"

"Your lease provides for overtime air conditioning at the cost of forty-five dollars per hour, and you must make the request by no later than 2 p.m. the same business day," answered the property manager who seemed to whisper when mentioning the forty-five dollar charge.

"Forty-five dollars per hour?" questioned William in a high-pitched tone. "That's an additional $1,800 per month just for air conditioning!" reiterated a stunned and agitated William.

Not the best retort, but Lily returned, "Actually that's $1,926 per month including sales tax."

Sadly, William ended up paying the additional $1,926 charges for overtime air conditioning to cool his space. The extra fans he brought to the office did not sufficiently cool the space.

I know. Some of you in more northern parts of the country are having a difficult time sympathizing with William who has to sweat a little while enjoying his ocean view. If you live in a city like Chicago or Minneapolis, the opposite would be true for you. Imagine having no heat in your office building during the winter and working until late in the evening.

"Igloo Office, may I h...h...help you?"

Business owners frequently overlook hours of operation when negotiating a lease. Let's address a few common misnomers about hours of operation that can negatively impact a business owner resulting in an Overwhelmed Business Owner.

Hours of Operation Misnomers

First, some LOI's omit the hours of air conditioning and overtime charges, leaving the subject to be addressed in the lease. Many business owners scrutinize proposals with greater detail than the lease document, as in William's case, and fail to realize the air conditioning hours.

Second, when a tenant is granted "24 hours/7 days a week access" to the space, it is often misunderstood to mean 24 hours/7 days a week air-conditioned access. This is not the case. Tenants *will* possess card key access to the building after hours and can enter their premises any time any day. Yet, the lease governs the specific times when landlords will provide air conditioning. Typical hours of operation are Monday through Friday 8 a.m. to 6 p.m., and half a day on Saturday, but vary from market to market.

Third, a full-service lease does not mean air conditioning is provided beyond the hours of operation. The everything-is-included concept of a full-service lease has its limits. The overtime air conditioning charges are paid for by each tenant and not included in the OPEX portion of the base rent. Should one tenant in a property require additional air conditioning, the other tenants in the property shouldn't be responsible for paying those charges.

Fourth, as Gana Mas learned, in South Florida, the office climate during certain times of the year will continue to be habitable without air conditioning (the opposite effect in colder regions). The winter months are typically cooler providing less heat load on properties allowing for a comfortable working environment long after the air conditioning shuts off. If touring space after hours during these months, be sure to request the standard hours of operation for the property, to not be surprised like William.

negotiation of the hours of operation is possible

Fifth, like most provisions of a lease, negotiation of the hours of operation is possible. Suppose your business requires air conditioning until 7 p.m. each work day, but the property's hours of operation shut off at 6 p.m., what can you do? The adage, "it never hurts to ask," most definitely applies. A business owner will never have more leverage than before signing a lease. The property owner wants to fill the vacancy. The leasing agent wants to close a deal and receive his compensation. Explain to the leasing agent you will need an extra hour of air conditioning each day of the work week or the space will not work. Landlords can get creative to accommodate the request. Perhaps the building systems permit the request for an additional hour with little to no consequence. The landlord may modify the deal (a slight increase in the rate or free rent period) to make up for the overtime air-conditioning charges. Perchance, there may be an existing tenant in the property already paying for the extra hour, and you can piggyback off the additional air conditioning.

Sixth, an NNN lease where a tenant pays for all the operating expenses for their space does not necessarily mean overtime air-conditioning charges are non-existent. In NNN offices leases, standard hours of operations often mirror full-service leases. The OPEX for the property including air conditioning is pulled together and then distributed to tenants based on their proportionate share.

Also, just because a utility company separately meters a space with the tenant paying their electric bill directly, that does not mean a tenant won't incur overtime air-conditioning charges.

Many HVAC systems within a space are connected to a cooling tower or a cooling water system which is regulated by the hours of operation in the lease. To run the cooling water system after hours requires additional electric and maintenance cost which will be passed directly to the tenant requesting the overtime air conditioning. In true NNN lease involving single occupant buildings, such as drug stores or bank branches, and certain retail and industrial properties, the entire HVAC system services a tenant's space exclusively. In such cases, a tenant may set its hours of operation and not incur overtime air conditioning charges.

A business owner must know the hours of operation of the property before signing a lease. If your business operates longer hours than an average work day, then properties that can accommodate or offer extended hours of operation should be considered. The overtime air-conditioning charges can quickly add up making a space unaffordable. It's very difficult to be a Triumphant Business Owner if you and your employees are too hot or cold in the office. William labored (sweated) through his five-year lease, but successfully negotiated an extra hour of air conditioning in his lease renewal.

Epilog - Closing Remarks

Don't Sign the Lease! The Tale of a Triumphant Business Owner expresses the answers I give to help business owners make wise, educated, and confident real estate decisions. I've endeavored to help Overwhelmed Business Owners become Triumphant Business Owners averting the common and costly mistakes when signing a lease—mistakes which you can easily avoid.

My firm's motto is "Why shouldn't YOU know as much about the transaction as we know? YOU sign the lease." As Solomon wrote in the book of Proverbs 19:2, *"Desire without knowledge is not good, and whoever makes haste with his feet misses the way"* (ESV). The word *desire* could also be translated *soul*. No business owner or decision maker should hurriedly sign a lease without knowing the ins and outs of what they are signing.

A lease will impact a firm's bottom line positively or negatively for many years. A poor lease will hamper a business' potential success in the same way a poor quarterback play or bad pitching will stunt the success of an all-star laden football or baseball team. At the same time, Triumphant Business Owners can confidently sign a lease which works for the advantage and benefit of their business maximizing their company's potential.

And *please:* Don't let a Bob, the Closer of the realty world keep you from working with a tenant advisor. I encourage you to consider the merits of a reputable and high-principled broker representing your best interest throughout the entire process from the kick-off meeting to the lease signing and move-in date. Find a Jason Woods.

Regarding landlords, I understand this book may seem one-sided. I have represented many notable and distinguished landlords who understand the needs of business owners. These landlords would acknowledge that a well-informed and represented tenant, that is a Triumphant Business Owner, is the best tenant. Better to settle questions and concerns during the lease negotiations, rather than after the lease begins.

I want to thank you for your time, consideration, and the investment you have made in your business by reading this book. We've spent a few hours together discussing the real estate business I've come to apprehend and value highly. I hope you learned something and enjoyed the book. Let me know your reviews and comments at www.dontsignthelease.com. If this book was helpful, pass it on to an OBO who can benefit as well. And please, if you find yourself in South Florida, look me up. I'd welcome an opportunity to discuss your real estate needs and share a *Cafecito*. Thank you.

Appendix A

Class A Property and Class B Property Characteristics

Below find a comparison chart of typical building features:

Property Features	Class A	Class B
New Construction	Yes	No
Nine-foot Ceilings	Yes	No
Quality Construction	Yes	Maybe
Covered Parking	Yes	No
Manned Security	Yes	Maybe
Quality Ownership	Yes	Maybe
Conference Facilities	Yes	No
Gym Facilities	Yes	No
Ground Floor Restaurant	Yes	No
Prime Location	Yes	Maybe
Valet Service	Yes	No
On-site Management	Yes	Maybe
Premium Views	Yes	Maybe
Efficient Floor Plan	Yes	Maybe
Prominent Lobby	Yes	No

Property Features	Class A	Class B
Expansive window line	Yes	Maybe
High-end Tenant Finishes	Yes	Maybe
Pets Allowed	No	No

The above group of features is not all comprehensive but offers a general overview of the differences between Class A and Class B properties. Please note, not every Class A property will offer all of the property features above.

Appendix B

Common Area Calculations

Common Area Factor* Calculation

$(RSF/USF) - 1 = Common Area Factor (CAF)$

RSF	USF	RSF/USF	CAF
10,000	8,500	1.176471	0.176471

Rentable Square Feet Calculation

$USF \times (CAF + 1) = Rentable Square Feet$

USF	CAF	CAF + 1	RSF
8,500	0.176471	1.176471	10,000

Usable Square Feet Calculation

$RSF / (CAF + 1) = USF$

RSF	CAF	CAF + 1	USF
10,000	0.176471	1.176471	8,500

*Please note: many terms can be used to describe the ratio between rentable and usable square feet. For the chapter, I used common area factor interchangeably with "add-on factor."

Other labels describing the ratio include loss factor, core factor, partial floor factor, full floor factor, etc. Each landlord and submarket may utilize slightly differing calculations.

Appendix C

How to Calculate a Parking Ratio

In chapter 3, there was an example in which a ten thousand-square-foot prospect reviewed two proposals with two different parking ratios. Property A offered a 4:1000 parking ratio while Property B offered a 3:1000 parking ratio. Below find a chart summarizing the steps to convert from parking ratio to parking spaces.

Property	Parking Ratio	Leased Space	Divide Leased Space by 1,000	Multiply Number by Parking Spaces: 1,000	Parking Spaces
A	4:1000	10,000	10,000/1,000 = 10	10 x 4 = 40	40
B	3:1000	10,000	10,000/1,000 = 10	10 x 3 = 30	30

Glossary

Assignment – An agreement between the original tenant and the new tenant in which the new tenant assumes all the liabilities and obligations of the master lease.

Base year – Typically, the base year is the year the lease begins. The operating expenses will be conjoined to the base year and compared to the base year operating expenses in future lease years to determine any increases.

Baseball arbitration – The process whereby an independent arbitrator determines whether the landlord or the tenant's definition of fair market rate is most accurate.

Boilerplate – A phrase describing standard provisions common in every lease.

Cap value – The value of a property an investor is willing to pay based on a compounded factor of the property's net operating income.

CBD – The Central Business District in a market, otherwise known as downtown.

Certificate of Occupancy – Also known as "CO," this is the final governmental approval establishing the completion of the tenant improvements allowing for the occupancy and use of the premises.

Class A - A property classified as Class A will provide more features and amenities than a Class B. See Appendix B for a list of features.

Class B – A property classified as Class B will provide fewer features and amenities than a Class A. See Appendix B for a list of features.

Common area factor – The proportionate or percentage share of the total of the common areas within the floor and the property that benefit the occupant space.

Common areas – All the floor and property areas outside the occupant space that benefit the occupant space.

Confidentiality agreement – An agreement between two parties not to disclose privy information, terms, and conditions of a property and/or a transaction.

Demising wall – Walls that separate a space from other tenant spaces and common area hallways.

Early access – A requisite in a lease providing for the right of a tenant to access the space early before the lease commencement to set up its FFE including phone and data lines.

Expansion Option – An option in the lease by a tenant to expand and lease identified space at any time at the tenant's sole discretion.

Expansion space – The space the landlord must make available to the tenant for expansion. If occupied, the landlord must relocate the occupying tenant to make the expansion space available.

FFE – Furniture, fixtures, and equipment which are the possession of the tenant and which the tenant is permitted to move out of the space when the lease expires.

Fiduciary – A relationship of loyalty and trust between a broker and his client where the broker is under contractual obligation to work for the best interest of his client.

FMR – The fair market rate is the base rental rate of the property and the submarket at the time the option to renew is exercised. The FMR is provided by the landlord and is typically subject to negotiations.

Full-service lease – A lease basis whereby the base rental incorporates all the operating expenses of the property. The all-inclusive base rent conjoins the property's operating cost to a base year. A tenant will pay for the proportionate share of increases in the property's operating cost above the base year operating cost.

Holdover tenancy – The occupancy of a tenant after the expiration of the term without a new lease in place resulting in penalties and fees to the tenant.

Hours of operation – The standard hours a property will operate at full capacity of services including when a landlord provides air conditioning or heating service to the space as defined in the lease agreement. Typical hours are business hours Monday through Friday and half a day on Saturday, excluding federal holidays.

HVAC – Heating, ventilation, and air conditioning.

Kick-off Checklist – An itemized list prepared by the tenant advisor mapping the order, course, and steps toward a lease signing.

Landlord – The property owner.

Landlord Consent Form – An agreement by the landlord to approve the sublease and/or assignment agreement.

Lease abstract – A summary of the main business points of a lease agreement.

Lease expiration – The date the lease agreement expires and the tenant's right to the space is null and void.

Leasing agent – The landlord's broker or leasing representative negotiating on behalf of the best interest of the landlord.

LOI – Stands for letter of intent which is the proposal between the landlord and the tenant containing all the business points to be negotiated.

Net operating income - The profit of a property owner derived by taking the base rent portion of the income less the operating expenses, real estate taxes and property insurance. Also, known as "NOI."

NNN lease – A lease basis in which the base rent and the operating expenses are fractured and billed separately. Also, known as a triple net lease, the tenant pays for all the operating cost of their space either directly or proportionately.

Operating expenses – The cost spent by a property owner to manage and maintain the property. Operating expenses include real estate taxes, property insurance, utilities, management fees, repairs and maintenance, and all other ancillary costs to operate the property. Also, known as "OPEX."

Option to Renew – A clause in the lease providing the tenant the absolute and complete right to renew the lease subject to the terms and conditions set out in the lease.

Overtime HVAC charge – The charge to the tenant for the use of air conditioning or heating after the hours of operation.

OBO – Overwhelmed Business Owner

P.I.G. – A Professional Income Generator, that is a real estate broker most interested in his commission above his client's need.

Parking ratio – The number of parking spaces the landlord will guarantee to the tenant per every one thousand square feet leased.

Personal guarantee – A legal obligation or written promise by a business owner to assume all the liabilities and obligations of a lease in the event of a default by the business entity that signed the lease.

Pre-tour phase – Before touring a space, this study will include a thorough review of current and future office space needs including size requirement, location, and budget.

Prior Written Notice Period – A condition of the Option to Renew Clause which sets a not-to-surpass date for when a tenant must notify the landlord in writing of their exercising the option to renew.

Property classifications – Property is classified based on standards within a given market and the perceived value of those standards.

Proportionate share – The percentage of space a tenant occupies within any given property. This percentage will be used to calculate the tenant's portion of the operating expenses.

Radon gas – A naturally occurring radioactive gas found in soil.

Radon Gas Disclosure Statement – By Florida Statute, a disclosure statement every lease document must include regarding radon gas.

Raw condition – A space that is unimproved either due to the property being newly constructed or a space that has been previously demolished.

REIT – Real Estate Investment Trust

Relocation Clause – A provision found in most leases affording the landlord the right to relocate a tenant to similar-sized space within the property.

Rentable square feet – The usable square feet plus the common area factor.

RFP – A Request for a Proposal prepared by the tenant advisor on behalf of the tenant commencing the negotiations and dictating to the landlord the specific terms and conditions to address in the proposal.

ROFO – Not dog speak, but rather a Right of First Offer. A ROFO requires a landlord to first offer available space to a tenant before offering the space to others.

ROFO Notice – The written notice provided by the landlord to the tenant delineating the terms and conditions by which the landlord will offer ROFO Space to the tenant.

ROFO space – The available space the landlord offers to the tenant. Typically, the ROFO space will be identified in the lease agreement.

ROFR – A Right of First Refusal requires a landlord to offer available space once a bona fide third-party offer is received and accepted for the space.

Second generation space – Space that has been previously built out or improved and ready for occupancy.

Shell or white-boxed space – Space that is in raw condition.

Short list – The properties selected from the tour list to consider further for negotiations.

Sublandlord – The original or master tenant of the lease.

Sublease – An agreement between the sublandlord and the subtenant where the subtenant will occupy and pay rent for the space with the sublandlord remaining liable for all obligations of the lease.

Sublease and Assignment Provision – A condition in the lease providing a tenant the right to find a replacement tenant for the space subject to the landlord's approval.

Substantially complete – The declaration by a landlord the tenant improvements have been completed, subject to punch list items, and the space is now ready for occupancy and use by the tenant.

Subtenant – The new tenant who will occupy the sublandlord's space and pay rent to the sublandlord.

Tenant – The business entity that signs the lease and is liable and obligated to abide by the terms of the lease.

Tenant advisor – A broker representing the tenant and negotiating on behalf of the best interest of the tenant.

Tenant Representation Agreement – An agreement between a tenant advisor and a tenant where the tenant acts as the exclusive broker for the tenant.

Term – The length of a lease agreement.

Termination fee – The fee the tenant must pay to the landlord as a condition to terminating the lease. The termination fee may consist of the landlord's unamortized cost including interest and a rent penalty.

Termination Option – A provision in the lease providing a tenant the right to preemptively terminate the lease before the defined expiration date of the lease.

TI – Acronym for Tenant Improvements which are the build-out or construction necessary to modify a space for a tenant's occupancy.

TIA – Otherwise known as Tenant Improvement Allowance representing the dollars a landlord will contribute toward the tenant improvements.

Tour list – The properties identified to tour as possible locations.

TBO – Triumphant Business Owner

Turnkey build-out – A build-out provision stipulating the landlord will perform and pay for all the tenant improvements subject to agreed upon plans and specifications.

Unamortized cost – The landlord's out of pocket costs that have not been recovered by the landlord during the term. Landlord costs can include tenant improvements, commissions and free rent.

Usable square feet – The space a tenant actually occupies or the tape measurement. Also, known as occupant space.

About the Author

Jorge L. Morales is a twenty-plus year commercial real estate veteran in the South Florida market. He spent ten years (2007–2017) as a vice president at the global real estate brokerage firm JLL (Jones Lang LaSalle, NYSE: JLL) before opening Blue Box Real Estate, LLC, (www.blueboxre.com) a different commercial real estate firm for business owners offering high level, trustworthy, and proven customizable real estate services to each client. Mr. Morales is also the founder of Don't  Sign the Lease, LLC (www.dontsignthelease.com) a business owner's forum designed to provide essential tools and helpful resources for business owners. Before his time at JLL, Mr. Morales served as a Leasing Agent and Director of Leasing with two regional real estate development and brokerage companies.

Mr. Morales has vast experience and knowledge of the office leasing sector on behalf of both landlords and tenants. Mr. Morales has represented over 3.5 million square feet of office space, including high profile institutional landlords as well as local and regional property owners. Mr. Morales has also served as a Tenant Advisor to many local, regional, and national tenants including universities and Fortune 500 companies.

Mr. Morales is a graduate of Florida International University. He resides in South Florida where he is happily married to his wife Diana and they are blessed with three children.